The Macat Library
世界思想宝库钥匙丛书

解析亚里士多德
《形而上学》

AN ANALYSIS OF
ARISTOTLE'S
METAPHYSICS

Aiste Celkyte ◎ 著

宫昀 ◎ 译

上海外语教育出版社
SHANGHAI FOREIGN LANGUAGE EDUCATION PRESS

目　录

引 言 ······ 1
    亚里士多德其人   2
    《形而上学》的主要内容   3
    《形而上学》的学术价值   4

第一部分：学术渊源 ······ 7
    1. 作者生平与历史背景   8
    2. 学术背景   12
    3. 主导命题   16
    4. 作者贡献   21

第二部分：学术思想 ······ 25
    5. 思想主脉   26
    6. 思想支脉   30
    7. 历史成就   34
    8. 著作地位   38

第三部分：学术影响 ······ 43
    9. 最初反响   44
    10. 后续争议   48
    11. 当代印迹   53
    12. 未来展望   57

术语表 ······ 61
人名表 ······ 66

CONTENTS

WAYS IN TO THE TEXT   73
     Who Was Aristotle?   74
     What Does *Metaphysics* Say?   75
     Why Does *Metaphysics* Matter?   77

SECTION 1: INFLUENCES   79
     Module 1: The Author and the Historical Context   80
     Module 2: Academic Context   85
     Module 3: The Problem   90
     Module 4: The Author's Contribution   96

SECTION 2: IDEAS   101
     Module 5: Main Ideas   102
     Module 6: Secondary Ideas   107
     Module 7: Achievement   112
     Module 8: Place in the Author's Work   117

SECTION 3: IMPACT   123
     Module 9: The First Responses   124
     Module 10: The Evolving Debate   129
     Module 11: Impact and Influence Today   135
     Module 12: Where Next?   139

Glossary of Terms   144
People Mentioned in the Text   149
Works Cited   153

引 言

要点

- 亚里士多德出生于公元前384年,一生中大部分时间在希腊雅典*度过。他在此地跟随柏拉图*学习,创建自己的学校,撰写作品。他于公元前322年去世。
- 《形而上学》对历史悠久的关于存在的本质的哲学理论提出了挑战,其中包括亚里士多德的老师柏拉图的理论。
- 哲学史上有许多关于柏拉图和亚里士多德理论孰优孰劣的争论。虽然今天二人的理论都没有绝对的相关性,但亚氏的作品仍旧为新一代哲学家的思想提供知识养料。

亚里士多德其人

亚里士多德于公元前384年出生在希腊城市斯塔吉拉,他是古代最重要的教师和哲学家之一。他的父亲是马其顿*王国(在古希腊北部边缘)的一名宫廷医生,曾教给他生物学和实证*研究,即通过观察或经验来获取知识。17岁时,亚里士多德来到雅典,进入阿加德米学园*,这是所由著名哲学家柏拉图建立的学校。亚氏在此处学习至公元前347年柏拉图去世。柏拉图本人曾跟随大哲学家苏格拉底*学习,这使亚里士多德得以获得当时顶尖的哲学智慧。

柏拉图去世后,亚里士多德回到马其顿宫廷,成为一个名叫亚历山大的9岁男孩的导师。这个孩子后来成为古代世界最强大的统治者之一:亚历山大大帝*。亚里士多德指导亚历山大直到他16岁。公元前335年,亚里士多德回到雅典,创建了自己的学校吕克昂学园*。在那里他写下了包括《形而上学》在内的大部分重要著作。公元前322年,他再次离开雅典,并于同年去世。

遗憾的是，亚里士多德的著作留存下来的很少。事实上，他去世后不久声名就消退了。直至约3个世纪之后，罗马编辑者安德罗尼柯*收集并出版了他的文章，他的著作才成为哲学研究的核心文本。《形而上学》这本书的标题，甚至命名了致力于研究存在的根本本质的哲学学科。但在亚里士多德去世后很久，安德罗尼柯才创造出"形而上学"*一词，可能仅仅用来指涉这本书在亚里士多德整体著作中的位置，它处于名为《物理学》的书之后（"meta"对应的希腊语单词为"在……之后"）。

《形而上学》的主要内容

在亚里士多德之前的几个世纪，探求本体论*——即对存在的本质的研究——的思想家们已经就到底何为"存在"提出理论了。早期的哲学家认为，"本体*"——即构成一切存在的事物——是气。有人认为是水，还有人认为是火，另有人认为是气、水、火、土这四种的混合。公元前4世纪，亚里士多德的老师柏拉图永远地改写了这项讨论，他认为独立存在于世界的永恒、无形的"理式"创造了我们所感知的现实，这就是柏拉图的理式论*。

尽管亚里士多德曾跟随柏拉图学习，但他却毫不犹豫地反对自己老师的这项结论。亚氏摒弃无形的（或非实体*的）理式概念，认为形式只在物质中显现。他指出柏拉图理论中的逻辑矛盾：如果任何对象都需要模仿理式才能存在，则人也要模仿人的"理式"，那么这个理式从何而来？这就引出了所谓的"第三人"*论证。

在《形而上学》中，亚里士多德主要探讨了他所谓的"存在之存在"*，"qua"意为"作为"。他也围绕其他一系列松散的观点，提出了相应的话题。亚里士多德分析了"潜在"与"实在"*等概念，据此回答了哲学家巴门尼德*在一个世纪前提出的哲学问题。从本质上看，巴门尼德的复杂论证认为，由于没有非存在的状态，因此变动在本质上是不可能的。亚里士多德通过区分作为潜在的存在和作为实在的存在来反驳他的观点。一个孩子，既是潜在的成人，又是实在的孩子。在亚里士多德看来，变动并不是从非存在向存在的转化，而是从潜在状态向实在状态的转化。

亚里士多德在《形而上学》中发展的另一个重要论点是"不动的动者"*，这是一种神圣的催化剂，是世间所有运动的源泉。"不动的动者"有多个还是仅一个，亚里士多德的结论并不明晰，因为在该书不同章节中他为每一个观点都给出了充分的理由。

亚氏通过强大的分析和观察来支撑自己的理论。他部分地接受了前人的研究成果，同时也颠覆了长期以来关于存在的本质的信条。他还为未来的哲学家提出了许多新的研究问题，这也是该著作始终占据哲学学科中心地位的原因之一。后辈哲学家们将继续讨论柏拉图式和亚里士多德式诠释的是非曲直。在某些方面，由亚里士多德思想所引发的讨论今天仍在继续，他作为哲学学科创始人之一的声誉也毋庸置疑。

《形而上学》的学术价值

在《形而上学》中，亚里士多德解决了一个他之前的哲学家争论了几个世纪的问题：什么是"存在"？这仍是形而上学研究的核心，亚里士多德约两千年前给出的答案也仍旧与该讨论相关。

亚里士多德有部分作品留存于世，但即使仅有《形而上学》一部，也足以确立他的声名。他的著作长期影响着各个时代的哲学家，从他所处的古希腊到罗马*时代，到中世纪基督教*和伊斯兰教*哲学家，直至今天。12世纪伊斯兰教哲学家阿威罗伊（伊本·路西德）*和13世纪基督教传教士托马斯·阿奎那*，都曾在著作中运用到亚里士多德的思想。18世纪苏格兰哲学家大卫·休谟*的观点是，从本质上看，没有证据的话，人无法确知任何事。他批评亚里士多德给出的关于本体的结论缺乏论据。休谟之后，亚里士多德的影响力式微。尽管如此，像今天一样，他的著作始终是学术体系的一部分。

20世纪下半叶，哲学家们重拾对形而上学的兴趣。如今的形而上学家关注的问题与亚里士多德时代已不相同，但学者们仍认可其著作的历史与哲学重要性。一些人通过注疏*（即分析和解释作品的文本）研究亚里士多德的《形而上学》和其他作品，以获知他的原意。还有一些人将这个古代文本视为获取新鲜灵感的源泉。他们调整亚里士多德的思想使之适应当代，并寻求扩展他的视野。例如，亚氏对本质属性和偶然属性的区分启发了现代的本质主义理论*。本质主义认为每个实体都有某些核心属性，以构成其身份和功能，似乎是绕了一圈又回到原地：本质主义理论挑战了休谟，休谟反驳亚里士多德，亚里士多德的思想又反驳休谟。

英国哲学家乔纳森·巴恩斯*指出："对亚里士多德知识遗产的描述，不亚于对整个欧洲思想史的描述。"[1]如今我们正恢复对亚里士多德著作的兴趣，这一遗产还将持续发挥作用。

---

1. 乔纳森·巴恩斯：《简明亚里士多德导读》，牛津：牛津大学出版社，2000年，第136页。

第一部分：学术渊源

1 作者生平与历史背景

要点 🗝

- 《形而上学》是哲学学科史上最重要的著作之一。
- 亚里士多德在雅典与其他哲学家接触的一段时期极大地影响了他的作品。
- 导师柏拉图对亚里士多德思想的发展尤为重要。

为何要读这部著作？

亚里士多德的《形而上学》是古典哲学最重要的著作之一，它由14篇论文构成，以希腊文字母命名，涉及多个形而上学主题。事实上，作为哲学子领域的形而上学的名称就来自该书的书名。

《形而上学》提出的核心问题是：什么是本体？哲学教授克里斯托弗·希尔兹*解释道，亚里士多德在该书中认为："对一切存在的研究是……可能的，只要它们与存在的核心范例相连。接下来去研究这个核心范例即可，也即本体。"[1] 亚里士多德在《形而上学》卷7中着重处理了本体问题，书中其他部分也或多或少涉及了这一话题，但它们主要关注的还是其他议题。例如：

- 对希腊哲学家苏格拉底以前时代（又称前苏格拉底时代*）哲学思想的解释和评估。
- 对哲学家柏拉图理式论的批评。理式论认为，与我们所感知到的质料世界比起来，无质料的理式或观念才是最根本的真实。
- 局部与整体之间的关系。对局部与整体进行研究来思考这样一个问题：是否存在某些复合对象（包含子部分的复杂对象），它的存在大于所有部分的总和。

亚里士多德在《形而上学》中提出的其他著名观点有：对变动的本质的讨论，认为宇宙中一切变动的第一原因是不动的动者：不动的动者使其他事物移动，它本身却不因任何先在的行动而移动。

亚里士多德对这些论题的分析极大影响了关于形而上学的讨论，这些讨论贯穿古代*（中世纪*之前但处于西方人类史之内的时代）、中世纪及之后的时代，甚至直到当代。任何人，如果希望学习哲学思想史或对形而上学中心问题进行广泛探索的话，从《形而上学》开始都是不错的选择。

> 苏格拉底去世后15年，亚里士多德出生在卡尔息狄斯半岛的小殖民地斯塔吉拉。他的父亲叫尼各马可，是亚历山大大帝的祖父阿明塔斯国王的宫廷医生。父亲去世后，亚里士多德于公元前367年迁居雅典并进入柏拉图的阿加德米学园，其时他17岁。此后20年，他一直是柏拉图的学生和同僚。可以肯定地说，在历史上其他任何时候，都没有如此智慧的头脑齐聚一处的现象。
>
> —— 安东尼·肯尼：《古代哲学：新编西方哲学史》

作者生平

公元前384年，亚里士多德出生在希腊小城斯塔吉拉，他先是跟随父亲学习生物学和实证研究（基于经验或观察获取知识），他的父亲是马其顿王国的宫廷医生。亚里士多德求学历程中最重要的阶段，是公元前367年迁居雅典并进入柏拉图的阿加德米学园之后。他在那里学习直到公元前347年柏拉图去世。

离开阿加德米之后，亚里士多德回到马其顿，为未来的国王和勇士亚历山大大帝授课。公元前335年，亚氏重返雅典，开办了自己的吕克昂学园，完成了包括《形而上学》在内的所有重要著作。"第二次在雅典逗留的那些年，是亚里士多德超乎寻常的多产期……我们今天所能读到的他的大部分哲学著作，差不多都写作于那个时期。"2

同大多数古代哲学家一样，亚里士多德生命的细节我们也所知甚少，但无疑雅典丰富的智识文化在他思想发展中起到了关键作用。

雅典是重要的政治中心，亚里士多德因此可以通过直接观察政治来发展他的政治思想。雅典也为形而上学研究提供了环境，其中像亚里士多德这样的思想家不仅能了解到多样的哲学观念，而且还可以通过哲学辩论观察这些观念如何被应用。因此，他接受的教育意味着他熟稔了随后在《形而上学》中批判和反对的观点，其中最重要的就是柏拉图的理式论。

创作背景

尽管是哲学界知名人士，亚里士多德的社会地位却有限，因为他不是雅典的全权公民。作为外邦人——希腊语中的"客籍民"*，他无法完全参与雅典的政治生活，不能拥有土地，还须缴纳比全权公民更高的税。我们能揣测的只有这些，而且恐怕正是他客籍民的身份，使他不得不在柏拉图去世后离开雅典。学者乔纳森·巴恩斯*描绘了一个可能的情景："公元前347年，希腊北方城市奥林索斯被马其顿军队攻陷，由演说家德摩斯梯尼*领导的雅典反马其顿势力方兴未艾。亚里士多德不是也从未是雅典公民，当时的情势较为微妙。"3 25年后，再次出现的反马其顿思潮迫使

他不得不在生命的最后时刻再次离开雅典。⁴

虽然对居住在雅典的外邦人的限制对亚里士多德有一定影响,他的作品中并没有反映出这一点。他所处的智识环境对哲学活动极为有利。他在柏拉图的阿加德米学园度过了 20 年时间,柏拉图本人又是苏格拉底的学生。如哲学教授安东尼·肯尼*所说:"……可以肯定地说,在历史上其他任何时候,都没有如此智慧的头脑齐聚一处的现象。"⁵

---

1. 克里斯托弗·希尔兹:"亚里士多德",《斯坦福哲学百科》,登录日期 2015 年 2 月 10 日,http://plato.stanford.edu/entries/aristotle/。
2. 克里斯托弗·希尔兹:"亚里士多德的哲学生命与写作",载《牛津亚里士多德手册》,克里斯托弗·希尔兹编,牛津:牛津大学出版社,2012 年,第 8 页。
3. 乔纳森·巴恩斯:"生平与作品",《剑桥亚里士多德导读》,乔纳森·巴恩斯编,剑桥:剑桥大学出版社,1995 年,第 4—5 页。
4. 巴恩斯:"生平与作品",第 6 页。
5. 安东尼·肯尼:《古代哲学:新编西方哲学史》,牛津:牛津大学出版社,2006 年,第 65 页。

2 学术背景

要点

- 形而上学处理与存在和现实相关的问题,也就是亚里士多德著名的主张"存在之存在",或作为存在的存在。
- 就像亚里士多德的老师柏拉图一样,前苏格拉底派哲学家都研究过根本的存在问题。
- 亚里士多德对形而上学传统的发展做出了重要贡献。

著作语境

亚里士多德并未为他的著作《形而上学》取名。他去世约3个世纪后,一位名叫安德罗尼柯的罗马编辑者收集亚氏的文章编成该书,并取了这个书名。为什么呢?通常的解释是,安德罗尼柯希望表达的意思是,这本书出现在亚里士多德写作《物理学》之后。Meta ta physica 这个希腊语词组的字面意思是"物理学之后"。

但也正由于安德罗尼柯,由亚里士多德著作催生的哲学子领域才能够以该著作命名。从广义上说,形而上学这门学科探讨关于生存、现实或存在本身的问题。亚里士多德写道:"这门科学探讨作为存在的存在……它与所有所谓的专门科学都不同;因为它们都不处理作为存在的存在这类普遍问题。"[1] 对"存在之存在"的研究成为定义形而上学学科的概念。我们可以将其理解为:"在某种意义上,这门科学完全是一般的或普遍的。与之相比,其他的专门学科每一门都只'截取'真实的一部分并加以研究……而叫做形而上学的这门科学,处理普遍意义上的存在问题。"[2] 自亚里士多德时代以来，形而上学涉及的都是对根本的生存或存在问题的研究，而不是针对特定对象或现象的研究。

> 在寻求解释的过程中，人们难免要遭遇困难……对亚里士多德来说，这些困难就是哲学的起点。靠着以自己的方式解决谜题或困难，他的哲学智慧渐长。因此，亚里士多德致力于写出一整本《形而上学》，就是罗列出围绕什么是真实的基本元素而产生的谜题。
>
> —— 乔纳森·李尔：《亚里士多德：理解的欲望》

学科概览

亚里士多德的《形而上学》以多种方式定义了它的领域，但该书也源出以往的哲学传统，如亚里士多德本人在《形而上学》卷1中所言，许多他之前的希腊哲学家都研究本体论问题，即存在的本质问题。英国哲学家安东尼·肯尼认为："多数论文从文献检索开始，试图表明迄今为止所有的著作都留有缺口，有待作者的原创性研究去填补。亚里士多德的《形而上学》也不例外……他推断出，最早的哲学在所有主题上都充满着含糊不清，因为这是它最初的婴儿期。"[3]

多数被亚里士多德视为前辈的思想家都是前苏格拉底派哲学家，其中最重要的一个派别是米利都*学派，它因其发源地米利都而得名。据对古代哲学的介绍指出，"泰勒斯*、阿那克西曼德*、阿那克西美尼*等来自小亚细亚米利都的第一批前苏格拉底派哲学家，都关心宇宙论*的提出，对我们生活的世界提出理性的解释。亚里士多德敏锐地观察到，他们专注于他所谓的质料原因，即世界

是由什么构成的问题。"⁴

亚里士多德发现米利都人提出的观点视野有限，但他也并非总是批评他们，其他的前苏格拉底派哲学家如恩培多克勒*则留给他积极印象。"亚里士多德称赞他认识到宇宙论并不仅是识别构成宇宙的元素，还包括分辨这些元素发展和混合的原因，以及它们如何构成这个生命与无生命复合物共存的实在世界。"⁵因此，前苏格拉底派思想为亚里士多德发展他的观点提供了肥沃的智识土壤。

学术渊源

有关亚里士多德一般意义上的智识生活佐证很少，已有信息还可能是矛盾的。其中存在矛盾的问题之一，是亚里士多德和以往智识传统的关系。一些研究认为亚里士多德极度傲慢，常以纡尊降贵的态度对待与他同时代和先前时代的哲学家。另有研究认为，亚里士多德敬重并关心他的朋友和同事。学者克里斯托弗·希尔兹推断说："我们应该承认一个明显的事实：在古代传记传统中，围绕着亚里士多德的负面评价都来自他的敌人的观点。他们被狭隘的嫉妒和竞争的狂热所驱使，无法凭借清醒的兴趣给出中立的评估。"⁶

对亚里士多德影响最大的人可能是他的老师柏拉图。他在柏拉图的阿加德米学园学习20年，因此有理由认为，亚氏与他老师的智识关系塑造了他自己思想的发展。但这并不是说他全盘接受了柏拉图的观点。事实上，亚里士多德以对柏拉图观点的批判而闻名。尽管我们无法确切说出柏拉图如何影响亚里士多德，但显然总体上影响是积极的。

学者乔纳森·巴恩斯认为："在亚里士多德的核心文本中，柏拉图的观点显然既是灵感的来源，也是困惑的来源（《形而上学》

最后两卷主要受柏拉图式数学概念的影响)。更模糊但更重要的是，亚里士多德整个的哲学兴趣都是由柏拉图的哲学兴趣塑造和决定的。"[7]

---

1. 亚里士多德：《形而上学》，威廉·大卫·罗斯译，载《亚里士多德全集》（牛津修订译本），乔纳森·巴恩斯编，新泽西州普林斯顿：普林斯顿大学出版社，1984年，第2卷第1584页。
2. 乔纳森·巴恩斯："形而上学"，载《剑桥亚里士多德导读》，乔纳森·巴恩斯编，剑桥：剑桥大学出版社，1995年，第69页。
3. 安东尼·肯尼：《古代哲学：新编西方哲学史》，牛津：牛津大学出版社，2006年，第3页。
4. 朱莉亚·安娜斯：《简明古代哲学导读》，牛津：牛津大学出版社，2000年，第100页。
5. 肯尼：《古代哲学》，第22页。
6. 克里斯托弗·希尔兹：《亚里士多德》，伦敦：劳德里奇出版社，2007年，第15页。
7. 乔纳森·巴恩斯："生平与作品"，载《剑桥亚里士多德导读》，乔纳森·巴恩斯编，剑桥：剑桥大学出版社，1995年，第17—18页。

3 主导命题

要点 🗝

- 在《形而上学》被构想的时代,哲学家通常会涉猎与存在的根本原理相关的问题。
- 在略早于亚里士多德的时代,当他的老师柏拉图发展理式论的同时,前苏格拉底派*质疑自然世界的运作。
- 通过运用略早时期思想家创造的概念,并对他们的某些观点和方法提出批评,亚里士多德的著作因此与此前的哲学传统产生关联。

核心问题

早在亚里士多德写作《形而上学》之前,关于本体的问题就引起哲学家之间热烈的争论。在《形而上学》卷7中,亚里士多德也指出:"无论现在还是过去,有一个问题总是被提出,它总成为大家质疑的主题。这个问题就是,存在是什么?或者说,本体是什么?"[1]

本体的哲学概念因具有许多细微差别而难以理解,但其核心意义却相对简单。我们可以将本体理解为"本体论*式的基本实体"[2]:即本体是对象的本质,与对象可能具有的任何偶然属性*相对立。例如,那些相信本体理论的人认为,人的本体不同于其体格属性,如苍白的皮肤、短翘的鼻子等。本体的概念描绘了对象存在中最为根本的部分。亚里士多德甚至声称:"本体是原理和原因。"[3]

对根本存在的兴趣,可追溯至早期的前苏格拉底派思想家泰勒斯、阿那克西曼德和阿那克西美尼，他们讨论了世界运作的原理。关于哪种自然元素承载着我们体验到的现实世界，每个前苏格拉底派思想家都有不同观点。例如，泰勒斯声称水是一切存在背后的基本原理。阿那克西美尼不同意，他认为是气。而阿那克西曼德则认为，是阿派朗*（无限），这种特殊的"无限"元素构成了世界。随后的前苏格拉底派思想家继承了这一传统。赫拉克利特*认为，世界受一个基于理性（逻各斯*）的原理所控制，他也称之为火。同时，恩培多克勒是第一位引入四元素（火、水、土、气）理论的哲学家。

关于本体论的讨论，也即对存在的本质的研究，在公元前4世纪的雅典发生了巨大变化，当时亚里士多德的老师柏拉图引入非实体的理式概念，称之为存在的原因。在所谓的中期对话录中，柏拉图论证认为，无形的*、永恒的、独立存在的理式能够解释一切现实。该理论后来改变了整个形而上学讨论的游戏规则，也为关于本体的本质的讨论带来重要创新。

> 事实上，无论现在还是过去，有一个问题总是被提出，它总成为大家质疑的主题。这个问题就是，存在是什么？或者说，本体是什么？
>
> ——亚里士多德：《形而上学》

参与者

柏拉图的形而上学本身在哲学史中就占有非常重要的地位，它也为理解亚里士多德的地位提供了一把必不可少的钥匙。可以说柏拉图最重要的创新是他的理式论。该理论假定理式作为因果实体而存在。

简单来说,柏拉图的著作区分了"存在"和"生成"。"生成"描述不断变化、易腐坏和不稳定的现实世界,而作为"存在"的理式,总是保持"相同并处于相同的状态。"[4] 此外,理式是"生成"的世界中属性的原因。柏拉图认为"生成"的世界中的对象参与*到理式中。如此一来,实在世界中的事物代表了它们各自的理式,同时它们也是"复制品"或源自理式的事物;但理式却不源自其他任何东西。因此,柏拉图常宣称只有理式是真正的存在。[5] 例如,一个美丽的人凭借参与美的理式而美丽,该理式构成什么是"美",而这个人是对该理式的某种反映。

这个复杂的理论有多重含义。如英国哲学家兼学者维里蒂·哈特*所解释:"理式在柏拉图的存在理论中发挥着作用:1. 理式是(基本的)存在(之一);2. 进一步看……理式除有着事物的某些特性外,也被确定为对事物负有因果责任。例如,美的理式对任何美丽之物的美负有因果责任。这样的话,理式本身并不仅是存在,它们还对世界某些其他方面的特性负有因果责任。"[6] 因此,"理式是柏拉图所谓的本体,因为一切事物的存在都源自它的理式。"[7]

当代论战

在《形而上学》中,尤其是卷 7、卷 13 和卷 14 中,亚里士多德批评了柏拉图关于本体的观点。柏拉图认为,理式既是无形的、永恒的、独立存在的物,也是存在的原因。亚氏对他的批评集中于此。根据柏拉图的观点,一个对象因参与美的理式而变美,美的理式代表的是完满的美和世界上所有美的起源。这意味着属性源自理式。亚里士多德却持不同观点:"如果我们以这样的立场看问题，显然没有任何普遍*属性是本体。另一显然的事实是，没有共同的谓词指向'这个'，而指向的是'这样的'。否则的话，就会出现很多困难，尤其会出现'第三人'。"[8] 亚里士多德的第三人论证认为，如果柏拉图的理式是存在的原因，则这些理式也需要它们的理式才得以存在。例如，一个人因表现人的理式而存在为人，但是为使人的理式存在则需要一个人的理式之理式，即第三人，以此类推。

亚里士多德认为，在讨论本体时，我们应当谈论对象本身而不是其偶然属性。亚氏在他自己的理论中抛弃了无形的、永恒的理式概念。他也用到了"形式"这一词，但是以与柏拉图相当不同的方式。他写道："所谓形式，我指的是每一物的本质和它的基本本体。"[9] 根据亚里士多德的说法，形式是固有的*，也就是说，只有当它展现在事物中时它才存在，但重要的是要认识到它的形成。本体是"形式在物质中的显现"，而不是形式和物质的复合。亚里士多德否定后一种情况，因为复合不可能是基本性的。[10] 这个哲学意义上严谨又创新的观点，使亚里士多德成为哲学史上最重要的形而上学家之一。

---

1. 亚里士多德：《形而上学》，威廉·大卫·罗斯译，载《亚里士多德全集》(牛津修订译本)，乔纳森·巴恩斯编，新泽西州普林斯顿：普林斯顿大学出版社，1984年，第2卷第1624页。
2. 迈克尔·J. 路克斯：《基本的"第一本体"：亚里士多德〈形而上学〉卷7和卷8解读》，纽约州伊萨卡：康奈尔大学出版社，1991年，第2页。

3. 亚里士多德：《形而上学》，第 2 卷第 1644 页。
4. 柏拉图：《智者篇》，尼古拉斯·P. 怀特译，载《柏拉图全集》，约翰·M. 库珀编，印第安纳州印第安纳波利斯和剑桥：哈科特出版公司，1997 年，第 269—270 页。
5. 柏拉图：《斐多篇》，G. M. A. 格鲁伯译，载《柏拉图全集》，约翰·M. 库珀编，印第安纳州印第安纳波利斯和剑桥：哈科特出版公司，1997 年，第 86 页。
6. 维里蒂·哈特："柏拉图的形而上学"，载《牛津柏拉图手册》，盖尔·法恩编，牛津：牛津大学出版社，2008 年，第 193—194 页。
7. 霍华德·罗宾逊："本体"，《斯坦福哲学百科》，登录日期 2015 年 2 月 10 日，http://plato.stanford.edu/entries/substance/。
8. 亚里士多德：《形而上学》，第 2 卷第 1640 页。
9. 亚里士多德：《形而上学》，第 2 卷第 1630 页。
10. 亚里士多德：《形而上学》，第 2 卷第 1625 页。

4 作者贡献

要点

- 亚里士多德批评柏拉图的理式论。该理论认为,本体在个体事物之外,它先于个体事物,比其更真实。亚氏则认为,本体是固有的形式,它显现在物质中。

- 亚里士多德关于本体的理论挑战了其时代公认的观点,为随后多个世纪的哲学家提出了一个极具影响力的可行的替代理论。

- 虽然亚里士多德借鉴了柏拉图的一些理论假设,但关于先存的概念,他提出了真正全新的观点。

作者目标

在《形而上学》中,亚里士多德声称他寻求关于"原因和原理"的知识。[1] 简言之,在该著作中他致力于探索最根本的本体论问题,也即对存在的本质的研究。

可以说,他在这部著作中提出的最重要观点是关于本体的理论。学者们通常将该理论解释为对柏拉图的回应,但它的重要性主要在于亚里士多德对本体大量而充分的阐释。若干世纪以来,学者们都将其视为对形而上学的关键性贡献。虽然亚里士多德可能认为他只是参与了一个业已充分发展的讨论,但他的理论本身成为杰出的哲学贡献。他关于本体是什么的有力论证,挑战了被广为接受的观点。

研究古代哲学的西奥多·斯堪瑟斯*教授解释道:"亚里士多德坚持认为,本体形式不是本体中更深一层的组成部分,而是组成部分中的另一本体类型。如此一来，亚氏展示给我们他自己理论的同时，也对柏拉图式*的形而上学提出批评。"² 在表明柏拉图的理式论关于本体的论述存在问题之后，亚里士多德提出了他本人完全不同的看法。亚氏没有（像柏拉图一样）视本体为超越物质世界的永恒、不变、无形的对象。他认为，本体是在物质中显现的一种形式，是所谓形式的内在性。亚里士多德通过有力的分析和敏锐的观察支撑自己的论证。

> 所有人都认为，所谓的智慧是应对事物的第一原因和原理。如前所说，这也正是为什么人们认为，富有经验的人比拥有某种感知力的人更有智慧，艺术家又比富有经验的人有智慧，工匠师傅比工匠有智慧，理论性知识比生产更具智慧的本性。显然，智慧就是关于一定原因和原理的知识。
>
> —— 亚里士多德：《形而上学》

研究方法

定义本体的过程中，亚里士多德声称他正在研究存在。他指出，哲学家以若干不同方式运用"存在"一词。他还论证称，基本的存在是本体，当我们谈论实质性存在时，应使之区别于以下的偶然属性*："当我们说一事物的属性如何时，我们说它好或者美，而不说它有三腕尺长或这是人；而当我们说它是什么时，我们不说它'白'或'热'或'三腕尺长'，而说这是'人'或'神'。"³

虽然亚里士多德的基本观点与柏拉图类似，他却以完全不同的方式进行研究。亚氏以周密、有条理的方法回答非常复杂的问题的本领无与伦比。"《形而上学》……运用亚里士多德最为复杂和有技术含量的构想,服务于整个哲学中一些最严苛、最根本的问题。"[4]

由于亚里士多德以技术化风格写作,还运用了许多额外概念和辅助调查来支持他对本体的有力描述,因此《形而上学》一直是出了名的难读。亚氏在他的作品中运用独特的方法,基于自己探索某物的想法来组织研究,"一开始是我们最熟悉的东西,然后转移至对依本性可知的第一原理的理解。"[5]

时代贡献

将亚里士多德对本体的描述置于他对柏拉图理式论的批评语境中,我们才能更好地理解它。柏拉图理论化了无形的普遍的物的存在,即理式,视其为所有存在对象的完美范例。亚里士多德批评了柏拉图的理式,指出该理论可能遭遇的各种反对声音,如所谓的第三人论证。亚氏的著名论证是,如果一个人因参与人的理式而成为人,则人的理式也需要另一理式才能成为人的理式,以此类推。[6]

然而,亚里士多德在他的作品中也使用了"形式"的概念。他认为本体是一种固有的形式,是在物质中的显现形式。亚里士多德重新诠释了对形式的存在的已有看法,并将其发展为一个独特的理论,"对柏拉图来说,关键点是断言这些理式的存在是独立的,同时它们又以某种神秘的方式'进入'以它们命名的具体事物中;而对亚里士多德来说,形式始终存在于实体之中。"[7]

我们从亚里士多德与柏拉图的交互中可见,虽然亚氏从已有传统中借用了某些概念,但他也为这些思想引入了真正全新的诠释。他之前的希腊哲学家已经研究过本体的概念,但亚氏的理论为这场辩论做出了重要贡献。他提出问题，并对形式等概念做出新的阐释，这些是从前的哲学家未能做到的。

---

1. 亚里士多德：《形而上学》，威廉·大卫·罗斯译，载《亚里士多德全集》（牛津修订译本），乔纳森·巴恩斯编，新泽西州普林斯顿：普林斯顿大学出版社，1984年，第2卷第1553—1554页。
2. 西奥多·斯堪瑟斯：《亚里士多德形而上学中的本体与共性》，纽约：康奈尔大学出版社，1994年，第72页。
3. 亚里士多德：《形而上学》，第2卷第1623页。
4. 克里斯托弗·希尔兹：《亚里士多德》，伦敦：劳德里奇出版社，2007年，第232—234页。
5. 艾伦·科德："亚里士多德的逻辑学与形而上学"，载《劳德里奇哲学史（第2卷）：从亚里士多德到奥古斯汀》，大卫·弗利编，伦敦：劳德里奇出版社，1999年，第54页。
6. 亚里士多德：《形而上学》，第2卷第1706页。
7. W.K.C.格思里：《希腊哲学家：从泰勒斯到亚里士多德》，伦敦：劳德里奇出版社，2013年，第121页。

第二部分：学术思想

5 思想主脉

要点

- 从广义上讲,《形而上学》的主题是"存在",尤其关注与存在相关的本体。
- 根据亚里士多德的说法,本体是物质固有的形式,它只存在于物质中。
- 亚里士多德的风格使他的复杂论证难以被人理解,《形而上学》作为整体的连贯性也为翻译问题所拖累。

核心主题

从广义上讲,亚里士多德《形而上学》的主题是存在。作者解释说,形而上学是"存在之存在"(作为存在的存在)的科学;作者还对他关于存在的探究和几何、物理等具体科学做了对比。[1] 如此他通过这个共同主题统领了《形而上学》各个章节。正如爱尔兰哲学家特伦斯·欧文*的解释:"无论所有这些章节的文学渊源是什么,它们都有一个共同主题,因为它们都为这门研究其他科学的共同前提的普遍科学做出贡献。"[2] 具体科学研究存在的特定方面;而亚里士多德的科学,特指如今的"本体论",则专注于存在本身。在《形而上学》中,亚里士多德通过对本体、变化、不动的动者概念的研究来讨论普遍的存在主题。

亚里士多德声称,对存在的研究相当于对本体的研究。[3] 有趣的是,只有《形而上学》的一些重要章节如卷7、卷8、卷9把本体作为主要主题来讨论。其他章节的内容,像卷3、卷4、卷6、卷12、卷13和卷14，通过关注与主题或多或少松散相关的话题作为对主题讨论的补充。卷5讨论哲学词汇，卷11包含对亚里士多德《形而上学》和另一著作《物理学》中观点的总结，但却没有以任何明显的方式涉及本体的主要讨论。

> 在该程式中，术语本身并不显现，但其含义却得到表达，这是每一事物本质的程式。
> —— 亚里士多德：《形而上学》

思想探究

我们可以将本体理解为"本体论意义上基本的物"[4]，也就是对象的本质。对亚里士多德来说，本体也是存在的原理和原因。[5]在《形而上学》卷7中，亚里士多德发展了形式质料说*理论。该理论认为本体是在物质中显现的一种形式。[6]该定义的叙述相当细致入微。通过反对本体仅是由形式和物质构成的复合物这一观点，亚里士多德指出，一个复合物不可能先于它的构成成分而存在。[7]真正的本体是一种形式，但它必须在物质中显现。因为，根据亚里士多德的说法，形式是固有的；也就是说，它们并非独立的存在，而只能在对象中找到。譬如，人的形式只能在人之中找到。

然而，这并不意味着每个人都有自己独特的形式。在亚里士多德看来，形式是一种本质，他认为："在该程式中，术语本身并不显现，但其含义却得到表达，这是每一事物本质的程式。"[8]研究亚里士多德的当代哲学家马克·科恩*指出，为更好地理解这个复杂定义，我们可将本质视为相当于一个对象所属的种。[9]在一个具体的人中显现的形式给了他作为人所必需的本质属性，但该形式并不能决定他的偶然特征,例如他鼻子的形状。

语言表述

亚里士多德现存的作品都以难读而出名。在《形而上学》中,他运用高度技术化、充满术语的语言,以简洁、厚重的散文形式来表现他非常复杂的观点。一个原因或许是,这些作品是他写给自己或者学生的授课讲义——"亚里士多德文集,如我们所知,似乎主要由与他的讲座紧密关联的著作构成。"[10] 任何学生,如果曾试图理解另一学生所做的笔记,都能体会亚里士多德带给我们的挑战。

《形而上学》还缺乏连续一致的叙事,这是导致读者认为该书难读的另一原因。书中的大部分章节,我们都可作为完整又独立的论文来读。关于亚里士多德如何或是否让独立章节之间的话题相互补充,学者们并未作出澄清。但与此同时,《形而上学》作为一个整体又具有某些连贯性,我们可将其视为通过不同路径研究与存在概念相关的各种问题的一个合集。正如20世纪古典主义者兼哲学家约翰·安克利尔*所描述的,亚里士多德的哲学"不是单一的、僵化的体系,那些论文也不能简单地按照时间顺序去排列和阐释。他作品真正的统一性在于方法、风格、智识特征,以及某些术语的无处不在。"[11]

亚里士多德在《形而上学》中使用的术语为哲学词汇的发展起到了作用。"后来哲学中的许多技术性词汇都源自亚里士多德形而上学术语的拉丁文版本,例如,'本体''本质''质量''数量'和'范畴'。"[12] 很多我们如今用来描述根本现实的术语都首先在《形而上学》中被界定和使用。由于这个及许多其他原因,该著作在哲学史上地位崇高。

1. 亚里士多德:《形而上学》,威廉·大卫·罗斯译,载《亚里士多德全集》(牛津修订译本),乔纳森·巴恩斯编,新泽西州普林斯顿:普林斯顿大学出版社,1984年,第2卷第1584页。
2. 特伦斯·欧文:"亚里士多德",载《简明劳德里奇哲学百科全书》,爱德华·克雷格编,伦敦:劳德里奇出版社,2005年,第56页。
3. 亚里士多德:《形而上学》,第2卷第1624页。
4. 迈克尔·J.路克斯:《基本的"第一本体":亚里士多德〈形而上学〉卷7和卷8解读》,纽约州伊萨卡:康奈尔大学出版社,1991年,第2页。
5. 亚里士多德:《形而上学》,第2卷第1643页。
6. 亚里士多德:《形而上学》,第2卷第1644页。
7. 亚里士多德:《形而上学》,第2卷第1624页。
8. 亚里士多德:《形而上学》,第2卷第1626页。
9. S.马克·科恩:"本体",载《亚里士多德导读》,乔治斯·阿纳格诺斯托普利斯编,马萨诸塞州莫尔登:威利-布莱克威尔,2009年,第203页。
10. 特伦斯·欧文和盖尔·法恩:《亚里士多德选读》,印第安纳州印第安纳波利斯:哈科特出版公司,1996年,第12页。
11. J.L.安克利尔:《哲学家亚里士多德》,牛津:牛津大学出版社,1981年,第4页。
12. 大卫·弗利:《劳德里奇哲学史(第2卷):从亚里士多德到奥古斯丁》引言,大卫·弗利编,伦敦:劳德里奇出版社,1999年,第4页。

6 思想支脉

要点 🗝

- 亚里士多德引入了"潜在"和"实在"的概念,以帮助他提出对巴门尼德变化悖论的解决方案。他还提出了第一原因和不动的动者的概念。
- 这些概念探讨了除本体外存在的其他方面,但它们自身也是非常重要的。
- 亚里士多德关于这些概念的想法,是对一些形而上学根本问题的典范式研究。

其他思想

亚里士多德在《形而上学》中处理的主要观点是本体。但"潜在"和"实在"等概念以及神的本质,也为他的"存在之存在"研究做出了贡献。[1] 亚里士多德在他的另一著作《物理学》中清晰地阐述了关于潜在和实在的观点。他运用这些概念回答哲学中的变化问题,该问题由前苏格拉底派哲学家巴门尼德提出。

在一个著名的复杂论证中,巴门尼德坚持认为,不能用非存在的概念去解释存在,因为非存在就不存在。最终,这使他断言,变化是不可能的,因为变化涉及状态的生成和毁灭。"巴门尼德反对多元主义,反对任何变化的现实:对他来说,一切都是不可分的、不变化的现实。任何与之相反的表现都是幻觉,会被理性和启示驱散。"[2]

巴门尼德和柏拉图(尤其他的中期著作)都不认可非存在的存

在，因此他们认为生成——从非存在变为存在——是不可能的。依照这个逻辑，由于毁灭是从存在到非存在的变化，因此毁灭也是不可能的。

在《形而上学》卷9中，为解决巴门尼德难题，亚里士多德通过区分潜在的存在和实在的存在对变化作了阐述。[3] 例如，一个孩子既是潜在的成人，也是实在的孩子。如亚里士多德所见，变化不是非存在变为存在的现象，而是"潜在的存在"变为"实在的存在"的现象。

> 一个实在在时间上总先于另一个实在，一直到那永恒的第一推动者。
>
> —— 亚里士多德:《形而上学》

思想探究

在《形而上学》卷9中，亚里士多德运用潜在和实在的概念来解释物质与形式的复合存在关系。据他所说，形式是实在，物质是潜在。[4] 例如，一块事实上的木头是雕像的潜在存在，因为雕刻家可以把它刻为雕像。亚里士多德认为，实在总是先于潜在的："一个实在在时间上总先于另一个实在，一直到那永恒的第一推动者。"[5] 这将我们引向《形而上学》中第二重要的观点：不动的动者这一主要概念。

在《形而上学》卷1中，亚里士多德指出神是第一原因和原理。[6] 他在卷12中阐释了这一想法。首先，亚里士多德将变化的本质作为一种运动来讨论。[7] 其次他研究了运动的类型，所以他或许能够确定所有运动的第一原因。他得出的结论认为："那么，某些物体始终随着无休止的、循环的运动而动;这显然不是理论上的,而是事实上的。因此,首先天堂必须是永恒的,而且也有移动它们的物体。而且由于被动和施动互为媒介,应有一个动者不被施动就可自行运动,它是永恒、本体和实在。"[8] 这个运动不是物理上的。不动的动者引发运动,就像被欲求的对象使欲求它的事物发生变化一样。[9] 亚里士多德随后又思考,不动的动者究竟有多个,还是唯一的。[10] 关于这一点他没有得出确切结论。哲学教授特伦斯·欧文指出,在《形而上学》卷12中,亚里士多德认为,每一个天体的运动都源自一个独立的不动的动者,但随后亚氏又宣称:"是一个唯一的、原初的、不动的动者把宇宙连结在一起。"这两种主张仍旧难以调和。[11]

亚里士多德关于变化和不动的动者的原创性和革新性观点,解决了他的时代已知的哲学问题;直到现在,这些观点仍为哲学辩论做出实质性贡献。

被忽视之处

亚里士多德的《形而上学》涵盖许多主题,包含多重论辩。这在某种程度上解释了它在各个时代受欢迎的原因。任何对形而上学及其历史感兴趣的人都会找到并研究这本书。在数千年的研究中,学者们没有太过忽视这部著作。它的中心主题如本体、变化、本质和神,以及亚里士多德的较小观察和推论,如对象可以大于它的组成部分之和等,[12] 所有这些都得到了精心的研究。

与此同时,亚里士多德在《形而上学》中涉及的某些主题仍有发现和重新诠释的空间。美国哲学家乔纳森·比尔*的著作《行与是:对亚里士多德〈形而上学〉卷9解析》,[13] 考察了亚氏在书中对"活动"和"能力"等术语的使用。简单来说,活动是实在,而能力是潜在。但亚里士多德对这些术语的使用方式非常复杂,导致难以给出它们精确的理论定义。通过细致研究亚氏使用这些术语的方法,以及他从理论上对这些术语进行描述的方法,比尔解决了《形而上学》卷9中主要的论证问题。

---

1. 亚里士多德:《形而上学》,威廉·大卫·罗斯译,载《亚里士多德全集》(牛津修订译本),乔纳森·巴恩斯编,新泽西州普林斯顿:普林斯顿大学出版社,1984年,第2卷第1584页。
2. 尼克·休格特:"芝诺悖论",《斯坦福哲学百科》,登录日期2015年2月11日,http://plato.stanford.edu/entries/paradox-zeno/。
3. 亚里士多德:《形而上学》,第2卷1656—1657页。
4. 亚里士多德:《形而上学》,第2卷1659页。
5. 亚里士多德:《形而上学》,第2卷1659页。
6. 亚里士多德:《形而上学》,第2卷1555页。
7. 亚里士多德:《形而上学》,第2卷1690页。
8. 亚里士多德:《形而上学》,第2卷1694页。
9. 亚里士多德:《形而上学》,第2卷1694页。
10. 亚里士多德:《形而上学》,第2卷1697—1698页。
11. 特伦斯·欧文:"亚里士多德",载《简明劳德里奇哲学百科全书》,爱德华·克雷格编,伦敦:劳德里奇出版社,2005年,第59页。
12. 亚里士多德:《形而上学》,第2卷第1650页。
13. 乔纳森·比尔:《行与是:对亚里士多德〈形而上学〉卷9解析》,牛津:牛津大学出版社,2009年。

7 历史成就

要点

- 在《形而上学》中,亚里士多德的主要贡献是对存在这一主题的一系列彻底且严谨的研究。
- 亚里士多德的路径和方法保证了该书的质量和它持久的声誉。
- 他关于本体的理论流行了近两千年,直到近代早期*(1450—1750)。

观点评价

在撰写《形而上学》时,亚里士多德的主要目的是探索最根本的本体论问题,即存在的"原因和原理"。[1] 但该书尚未完成时,他就去世了,这导致该书略显杂乱,缺乏清晰的结构。书中卷3、卷4、卷6、卷7、卷8和卷9清楚地探讨本体论话题,尤其是存在问题。其余部分处理的话题显然并不属于本书的主要论述。

今天我们读到的书中各卷的顺序,并不是亚里士多德排列的。在亚氏去世约3个世纪后,罗马编辑者安德罗尼柯收集了他在相关话题上的论文,并以《形而上学》之名出版。因此,我们不知道亚里士多德想要他的成书实现什么目标。很有可能他希望对所有现存事物的根本本质进行研究,由此引入并发展出对哲学根本问题的彻底理解:如什么是本体,如何解释变化,如何理解第一原因。

《形而上学》中的思想确实具有一定的概念统一性,所有章节都包含与形而上学有关的讨论。虽然亚里士多德的论证不总是清晰地相互关联，但《形而上学》仍是引人注目的关于存在之本质的研究合集。

就亚里士多德着手解决并提出关于存在的论述而言，他的作品仍非常成功。他不但处理一些最为复杂的形而上学问题，还试图给出可能的答案。亚氏强大的、令人信服的本体论阐释可以与当时柏拉图式的形而上学相媲美，并且多个世纪以来被认为是对形而上学的重要贡献。亚里士多德的译者乔·萨克斯指出："当亚里士多德在我们所知的《形而上学》一系列文章中阐述他的中心问题时，他指出这是一个不断向自身发问的问题。他是对的。他把自己对处理这个问题所做的贡献，视为属于对它的回应的最终阶段。我认为这一点上他也是对的。《形而上学》是最有帮助的书之一。它始终在应对一个问题，该问题的提出是使我们人之为人的原因之一。"[2]

> 当亚里士多德在我们所知的《形而上学》一系列文章中阐述他的中心问题时，他指出这是一个不断向自身发问的问题。他是对的。他把自己对处理这个问题所做的贡献，视为属于对它的回应的最终阶段。我认为这一点上他也是对的。《形而上学》是最有帮助的书之一。它始终在应对一个问题，该问题的提出是使我们人之为人的原因之一。
>
> ——乔·萨克斯："亚里士多德：形而上学"

当时的成就

在亚里士多德一生中及我们的时代，《形而上学》一直很受欢迎，就像他的其他作品一样。一些学者过去常争辩，亚氏的亲密追随者去世之后，他的著作几乎完全被遗忘，直到罗马时代它们才被重新出版。当代学者则普遍认为，亚里士多德的观点在整个希腊化时代*始终广为人知。希腊化时代指亚历山大大帝死亡至古罗马帝国崛起之间的 3 个世纪。[3]

《形而上学》对早期伊斯兰教哲学家影响也很大。重要的思想家们，如 12 世纪初的法律学者兼哲学家阿威罗伊（伊本·路西德）撰写了对亚里士多德作品的评论，并将亚氏的观点用在他们自己的著作中。亚里士多德和其他古代哲学家在中世纪早期（开始于 12 世纪）几乎不为人知，他的作品在欧洲是逐渐被广泛接受的。亚氏作品的再次出现在欧洲思想家中引发了极大兴趣。

亚里士多德《形而上学》中的主要话题——本体——自他首次讨论以来，始终是经典的形而上学概念和该学科关注的中心。古代和中世纪的哲学家都认为《形而上学》是重要作品。亚里士多德关于本体是显现在事物中的形式的论述，能够媲美早些时候柏拉图的观点。柏拉图认为，本体必须是存在于有形世界之外、无形的、永恒的理式。古代和中世纪的形而上学家就柏拉图和亚里士多德对本体的不同论述进行辩论，将这两种观点用作构建自己思想的参照点。这就是为什么许多世纪以来，《形而上学》始终是哲学辩论中的核心。

局限性

人们可能会将《形而上学》描述为它的时代的产物，因为它关注的是与古典时期*哲学家最相关的主题。但在亚里士多德完成它之后的许多个世纪里，它仍然是一部重要的作品。

然而在现代时期，18 世纪苏格兰哲学家大卫·休谟*提出的批评挑战了这部作品的相关性。休谟认为，因为亚里士多德关于本体的概念没有任何论据可依，哲学家们应该丢弃它。取而代之地，休谟提出了一个所谓的束理论*：对象的本质是它们所有属性的总和。[4] 亚里士多德认为，一个人的某些特定属性，比如翘鼻子或身高，不能解释人是什么的问题。然而休谟却持完全相反的态度。这种批评并未从哲学辩论中完全抹杀亚里士多德，但它的确很大程度上削弱了亚氏的影响力。更重要的是，哲学讨论的焦点发生了转移。伴随休谟对本体概念的反驳，哲学家开始探究阐释何为存在之本质的其他路径。最终，学者们开始将亚里士多德的思想归入"哲学史"中，《形而上学》和他的其他著作不再出现在学科的前沿地带。

---

1. 亚里士多德：《形而上学》，威廉·大卫·罗斯译，载《亚里士多德全集》（牛津修订译本），乔纳森·巴恩斯编，新泽西州普林斯顿：普林斯顿大学出版社，1984年，第2卷第1553页。
2. 乔·萨克斯："亚里士多德：形而上学"，因特网哲学百科全书，登录日期2015年2月10日，http://www.iep.utm.edu/aris-met/。
3. 乔纳森·巴恩斯："生命与著作"，《剑桥亚里士多德导读》，乔纳森·巴恩斯编，剑桥：剑桥大学出版社，1995年，第10—11页。
4. 参见，例如，大卫·休谟：《人性论》1.4.6.3。

8 著作地位

要点

- 亚里士多德写作了大量论文,所涉话题范围很广。
- 在《范畴篇》和《物理学》两部著作中,他也对《形而上学》的中心观点进行过思考。
- 《形而上学》仍是亚里士多德最著名和最重要的著作之一。

定位

亚里士多德什么时候写作了《形而上学》?学者们对该问题进行了广泛的讨论。直至20世纪,学术界仍认为亚氏的著作是一个连贯的、完成性的整体,并把整个文集看作一个成熟思想家的产物。然而过去100年间,学者们挑战并普遍否认了这一观点。20世纪初研究亚里士多德的哲学家托马斯·凯斯*认为,亚氏一定花费了多年时间才完成他的全部著作,因此不可能所有著作都是在他生命末期完成的。相反,凯斯认为亚里士多德以手稿的形式保存他的著作,并在整个学术生涯中不断地对它们进行完善。[1]

《形而上学》中各卷之间统一性的缺乏也支撑了这一解释。多样的主题以及它们之间连贯性的缺乏,清楚表明亚里士多德不是以传统的方式——短时期完成全书的书写——写作《形而上学》的。它很有可能是在更长一段时间内撰写的。著名亚里士多德研究学者乔纳森·巴恩斯指出,根据《形而上学》古代评论的暗示,亚里士多德去世前没有对该书进行合理的编排,它当时处于一种不连贯状态。[2] 总的来说,学者们倾向于认为,《形而上学》是贯穿亚里士多德一生的一些相关联作品的结集，但在去世前他确实没有把它完成。

《形而上学》中发展的中心主题，即本体的概念，在亚里士多德另一部著作《范畴篇》中也可以找到。尽管没有清晰的证据表明《范畴篇》的写作先于《形而上学》，"但如果假设《形而上学》第 7 卷写得略晚，则我们更容易理解《范畴篇》中的本体学说与《形而上学》第 7 卷中该学说的关系。"[3] 学生们常在《形而上学》之前先读《范畴篇》，作为对本体概念的导入，因为后者中的观点略微简单。譬如，在《范畴篇》中，亚里士多德对本体的定义是它可以接收对立面，并在数量上保持单一。[4] 为帮助读者理解这个观点，亚氏举出一例：由于颜色不可能既黑又白且还保持为同一种颜色，因此颜色不是本体。但人可以从苍白到被晒黑仍保持为同一个人，因此人之为人是一种本体。这个观点表明，我们必须把本体理解为对这是什么——如人是什么——的解释。在《范畴篇》中，亚里士多德指出，如果想了解人之为人的本质，我们不能只看人有什么属性。一个人可以苍白、年老且是雅典公民，但人苍白、年老且是雅典公民都不能解释人之为人的本质。为此，亚里士多德建议，为确定人的本体是什么，我们应审视一个人历经所有变化始终不变的是什么。

> 亚里士多德是一位出色的研究者和作家。他留下大量著作，可能有大约两百篇论文，其中现存的约有三十一篇。
>
> —— 克里斯托弗·希尔兹："亚里士多德"，《斯坦福哲学百科》

整合

"亚里士多德是一位出色的研究者和作家。他留下大量著作，可能有大约两百篇论文，其中现存的约有三十一篇。"⁵ 虽然我们只拥有亚里士多德作品相对较小的一部分，但那些幸存的文本涵盖了从形而上学到政治学的广泛主题。即使在经常写作大量话题广泛的论文的古代哲学家中，亚氏的成就也令人瞩目。

亚里士多德作品所涉范围也可以帮助我们理解他更为复杂的观点。学者和哲学家们通常会阅读和交叉引用他的一系列著作，如《物理学》《范畴篇》（有时还包括《论灵魂》）以及《形而上学》。"《范畴篇》和《物理学》中的一些基本概念，包括本体、特定、普遍、形式、物质、原因和潜在等，都在《形而上学》中得到了更充分的讨论。"⁶ 在试图理解《形而上学》中的观点时，我们应当把其他著作中涉及相同或相似话题的讨论纳入考量范围。我们还可以把他的不同著作一起阅读，找出他对一些普遍问题的整体立场。例如，如果要了解他关于人的本质的观点，我们不仅要读《形而上学》或《论灵魂》，还可以读一读《尼各马可伦理学》和《政治学》。

意义

亚里士多德写了许多在哲学各个领域具有开创性的论文，《形而上学》是其中最重要之一。亚氏创新性的思维方式使他的整体著作对后世哲学家产生极大影响。但即使只写过《形而上学》一部，也足以确立他对哲学史的巨大影响。受亚里士多德的追随者逍遥派*的接受和传播，《形而上学》中的观点回响了多个世纪。从古希腊和古罗马哲学家，到中世纪思想家和伊斯兰教知识分子，再到现代哲学家，许多人都研究其中的观点。

但是，由于哲学学科的发展，自始于15世纪中叶的近代早期开始，亚里士多德的影响力日渐式微。哲学家很大程度上反对本体这一话题的讨论。这不仅因为新的理论和思想的出现，还因为哲学关注的焦点开始转向不同话题，因此这也降低了亚里士多德的相关性，但并未减弱他的总体成就。即使哲学家不再接受亚里士多德的某些观点和讨论，他仍是哲学史上最伟大的思想家之一。学者们仍在讨论亚氏思想某些方面的历史和哲学重要性。《范畴篇》与《物理学》，尤其是《形而上学》，使亚里士多德获得认可，并成为西方哲学中最重要的形而上学家之一。

---

1. 托马斯·凯斯："亚里士多德"，载《亚里士多德的哲学发展：问题与展望》，威廉·韦恩斯编，马里兰州拉纳姆：罗曼与利特尔费尔德出版社，1996年，第13页。
2. 乔纳森·巴恩斯："罗马的亚里士多德"，载《哲学世俗剧II：柏拉图和亚里士多德在罗马》，乔纳森·巴恩斯和米里亚姆·格里芬编，牛津：克拉伦登出版社，1997年，第61—62页。
3. 特伦斯·欧文："亚里士多德"，载《简明劳德里奇哲学百科全书》，爱德华·克雷格编，伦敦：劳德里奇出版社，2005年，第51页。
4. 亚里士多德：《范畴篇》，约翰·L.安克利尔译，载《亚里士多德全集》(牛津修订译本)，乔纳森·巴恩斯编，新泽西州普林斯顿：普林斯顿大学出版社，1984年，第1卷第7页。
5. 克里斯托弗·希尔兹："亚里士多德"，《斯坦福哲学百科》，登录日期2015年2月10日，http://plato.stanford.edu/entries/aristotle/。
6. 欧文："亚里士多德"，第56页。

第三部分：学术影响

9 最初反响

要点 🔑

- 普罗提诺*批评亚里士多德的观点,声称亚氏未能将事物的偶然属性包含在本体概念之中,这导致人们无法区分单个事物的本体。
- 阿弗罗狄西亚的亚历山大*等评论者支持亚里士多德的观点,反对亚氏的敌对派别比如斯多葛派*的观点。
- 总体上,亚里士多德的思想很受欢迎,启发了许多哲学家发展他们自己的思想。

批评

在《形而上学》中,亚里士多德批评当时的哲学传统。但令人惊讶的是,他自己却很少受到明确的批评。在他最亲密的圈子里,他的追随者——被称为逍遥派——似乎更有兴趣保护他的著作,而不是与之进行论战。有趣的是,这种趋势甚至持续到亚氏最初的吕克昂学园解散之后。在古代晚期,亚里士多德的著作颇受阿弗罗狄西亚的亚历山大等评论者欢迎,他解释了亚氏的观点,批评了亚氏竞争对手的哲学论述。

甚至是认同柏拉图思想的新柏拉图主义者*,都没有彻底反对亚里士多德的形而上学,他们通常把它与柏拉图的著作放在一起研究。研究古代哲学的当代学者义赛托特·哈多特*认为,新柏拉图主义哲学家发现,柏拉图和亚里士多德的著作可以放在一起来研究,但"柏拉图的哲学,与亚里士多德的相比,被认为更高尚、更具神学性、更给人启发。同样清楚的是,《形而上学》位于一个中间阶段,它处在对自然原理、原因的研究和柏拉图在他的《巴门尼德篇》中发展的真正的神学中间。亚里士多德的思想从本质上讲,并不是彻底'超验的'。"[1]

这股潮流中有一个突出的例外,即普罗提诺在他的开创性著作《九章集》中对亚里士多德本体概念的批评。普罗提诺运用多种论据,批评亚氏认为本体是固有的*形式在物质中的显现这一观点。同时,他捍卫柏拉图式*的认为理式的存在是超越我们可视、可感的感性世界的这一定义。著名古代哲学专家劳埃德·格尔森*指出,普罗提诺在亚里士多德对本体的论述中发现一个问题,他认为亚氏不能合理地保证本体是对象固有的。如果我们假设偶然属性(例如有一个翘鼻子)不是本质的一部分,则本质中没有什么是属于一个特定对象的。例如,这样一个本质的概念就无法区分柏拉图和苏格拉底。因此,在普罗提诺看来,这导致亚里士多德对本体的论述站不住脚。[2]

> 柏拉图的哲学与亚里士多德的相比,被认为更高尚、更具神学性、更给人启发。同样清楚的是,《形而上学》位于一个中间阶段,它处在对自然原理、原因的研究和柏拉图在他的《巴门尼德篇》中发展的真正的神学中间。亚里士多德的思想从本质上讲,并不是彻底"超验的"。
> ——义赛托特·哈多特:"根据对《范畴篇》的新柏拉图主义评论的前言讲授哲学时亚里士多德评论的作用"

回应

亚里士多德没有机会回应当时对《形而上学》的批评,现有证据表明大部分批评出现在他去世之后。他一生中很有可能参与了许多批判性辩论，甚至可能为回应批评而改变了自己的观点，但关于这一点没有留下证据。证据的缺乏使我们无法绝对地知晓亚里士多德是如何被批评的，这些批评又对他造成了什么影响。

亚里士多德去世后，通常被称为逍遥派的追随者们承担了推广他的思想和回应对他的批评的任务。如，逍遥派评论家阿弗罗狄西亚的亚历山大写过关于《形而上学》的评论，他支持亚氏的观点，反对其他哲学流派如斯多葛派的思想。亚里士多德的支持者也回应了那些探讨柏拉图和亚里士多德思想区别的人。

然而，这些评论者不一定是对针对亚里士多德的批评做出回应的，他们只是涉及一些不同的理论，就像其他派别也会提到他们一样。例如，斯多葛派思想并没有批评甚至没有清晰提及过亚里士多德。但这些保护亚氏使之免受潜在的或明显的批评的评论，却使得他的思想在其作品出版很久以后仍具有相关性。

冲突与共识

自古代以来，亚里士多德在《形而上学》中提出的观点就被广泛地阅读、讨论和争辩。哲学家们认为，柏拉图主义*能与亚里士多德著作中的哲学相媲美。话虽如此，但即使是柏拉图派思想家或有其他哲学倾向的人都赞赏《形而上学》。无论在亚里士多德时代还是之后，柏拉图主义者的批判性辩论都未能必然影响该著作的接受。我们可以把柏拉图主义和亚里士多德主义之间的竞争，理解为对这两个流派思想优劣的持续性讨论。辩论双方没有任何人完全地否定过对方的理论。

许多重要思想家都对受亚里士多德启发的形而上学给予了有趣的支持。根据加拿大哲学家克劳德·帕纳乔*的说法，13世纪传教士托马斯·阿奎那"反对柏拉图主义,因为它错误地认为,普遍性必须以独立的方式存在于精神以外的世界,并与精神相隔离……尽管从严格意义上讲普遍性只存在于他的思想中,然而它们在单个事物中有着外部基础:人的本质以某种方式存在于单个的人中。"[3]

帕纳乔的现代研究表明,亚里士多德的观点在其去世后几个世纪里仍被谈论和探讨。在赞同亚里士多德思想和支持柏拉图或新柏拉图理论的思想家之间,一场激烈的辩论仍在进行。尽管有的思想家宣称坚决反对亚里士多德的形而上学阐释,但随后又会有哲学家复兴并捍卫它,使得它能启发出新的思想。

---

1. 义赛托特·哈多特:"根据对《范畴篇》的新柏拉图主义评论的前言讲授哲学时亚里士多德评论的作用",《牛津古代哲学研究》增刊,1991年,第184页。
2. 劳埃德·格尔森:《普罗提诺》,伦敦和纽约:劳德里奇出版社,1994年,第93—96页。
3. 克劳德·帕纳乔:"中世纪形而上学1:普遍性的问题",载《劳德里奇形而上学指南》,罗宾·列·普瓦德万等编,伦敦和纽约:劳德里奇出版社,2009年,第52页。

10 后续争议

要点 🗝

- 亚里士多德的《形而上学》在托马斯·阿奎那和阿维森纳（伊本·西拿）*等后世思想家的著作中发挥着重要作用。
- 亚里士多德的追随者逍遥派形成了一个思想流派，但它的存续并没有超过希腊化时期。
- 《形而上学》在以该书命名的学科的发展中发挥着重要作用。亚里士多德著作引入的新想法和新论点居于学科的中心位置，激发各流派的哲学家继续构建他们自己关于这些话题的研究。

应用与问题

亚里士多德的《形而上学》极大地影响了整个哲学，尤其是被命名为"形而上学"的学科的演变。他对柏拉图本体是无形的理式这一观点的批评，在形而上学发展中起着尤为重要的作用。

对新柏拉图主义者或中世纪形而上学家等后世哲学家来说，柏拉图式和亚里士多德式的关于本体的论述显示出一个巨大的困境。柏拉图认为本体是无形、永恒的理式；亚里士多德则认为本体只存在为固有的形式，即在事物中显现的形式。哲学家认为两种论述都很重要，双方的矛盾至今也无法调和。这种不相容性在思想家中引发激烈的辩论。一些人信奉其中一方的观点，捍卫它并反对另一方。另一些人选择回避问题，以全然不同的方式发展出处理存在问题的论述。如英国哲学家大卫·塞德利*所指出："自公元2世纪到至少文艺复兴*结束，柏拉图主义和亚里士多德主义始终是西方传统中的主导性哲学，它们的知识遗产在当今西方哲学中仍占据中心地位。"[1]

亚里士多德思想对伊斯兰教哲学传统也非常重要。他的形而上学影响了10世纪波斯医学家伊本·西拿（或拉丁名阿维森纳）等许多杰出的思想家。同其他伊斯兰教哲学家一样，伊本·西拿将《形而上学》视为关于本体论的奠基性著作。他还运用亚里士多德的本体等概念，发展出他自己的原创性思想。伊本·西拿写过三部百科全书，其中第一部名为《论治疗》(al-Shifa)，"仿照了该哲学家即亚里士多德的文集，涵盖了自然科学、逻辑学、数学、形而上学和神学。"[2]

中世纪的欧洲哲学家也将《形而上学》视为基础性文本，探讨柏拉图主义和亚里士多德主义的区别，以及它们各自不同的关于本体的本质的观点。中世纪形而上学家通常采纳二者中一方的论述，并基于此建立他们自己的思想。受亚里士多德影响的最著名的中世纪哲学家，大概是13世纪意大利传教士托马斯·阿奎那，"阿奎那哲学每一部分都充满着形而上学原理，其中许多显见是亚里士多德式的。因此，诸如潜在与实在、物质与形式、本体、本质等概念，都是阿奎那形而上学的根本，也都应被置于它们本来的亚里士多德语境中进行考量。"[3]

包括《形而上学》在内的亚里士多德著作至今仍影响着哲学家们，对那些认为本体或本质属性不同于偶然属性的人来说，其影响力尤甚。

> 自公元2世纪到至少文艺复兴结束，柏拉图主义和亚里士多德主义始终是西方传统中的主导性哲学，它们的知识遗产在当今西方哲学中仍占据中心地位。
> ——大卫·塞德利："古代哲学"，《劳德里奇哲学百科全书》

思想流派

亚里士多德自己的哲学学校吕克昂学园存续时间很短。他的著作包括《形而上学》在内，最初都只是在他的学园里被阅读。但大约3个世纪之后，罗马编辑者安德罗尼柯将它们结集并出版。在此期间，亚里士多德受到的关注少于他活着时，是安德罗尼柯对他著作的出版重新唤起人们对其思想的兴趣。

公元前322年，亚里士多德去世之后，他的追随者逍遥派继续运营吕克昂。但后来他们认为自己最重要的任务是保护亚里士多德的学术遗产，并在他的思想传统中继续做研究。如著名的亚里士多德研究学者罗伯特·沙普尔斯*所言，早期逍遥派最关心的是从多个研究领域收集信息并解决理论难题。该流派在希腊化时代就不大流行了，但一直存续至公元前1世纪罗马人征服雅典时。

对亚里士多德思想的第二波兴趣发生在约300年之后的罗马时代，可能就是安德罗尼柯出版亚氏著作的时代。那个时代对他著作的评论越来越多，显示出亚氏对新一代哲学家的影响力。那些人中有作品留存的，其中之一是著名评论家阿弗罗狄西亚的亚历山大，他专事撰写关于《形而上学》的文章。

古代之后、中世纪之前一段时期的西方文明中，在由亚里士多德思想建立的哲学背景下，哲学家却不太经常讨论他的观点。相反地，思想家们将亚氏引入的概念应用进各式各样的哲学问题中。我们不能称这些后世思想家为亚里士多德的"追随者"，但他的著作的确在他们发展自己的思想时产生了影响。譬如，中世纪逻辑学家（研究逻辑学或擅长运用逻辑的人）运用亚里士多德物质和形式的概念解释三段论，该逻辑推理由两个一般陈述推出一个较为特殊的陈述。[4]

爱尔兰哲学家特伦斯·欧文认为："对亚里士多德的现代历史研究始于 19 世纪，它带来对哲学的重新评估，亚氏的作品也又一次成为哲学见解和论证的来源。亚里士多德哲学的许多主题，如本体的本质、形式和物质的关系等，又一次出现在哲学辩论问题中，亚氏对这些辩论的贡献影响了哲学讨论的进程。"[5]

当代研究

总体来说，亚里士多德的《形而上学》在当今的哲学家、哲学史家和知识分子中都享有很高的声誉。当代思想家常运用《形而上学》中的思想启发他们自己的理论。学者们还运用注疏的方式解析《形而上学》，通过批判性分析和细致研究得出它的原意。无论他们解读《形而上学》的目的是什么，该著作始终非常重要，不仅对以它命名的学科发展，而且对它作为一部哲学著作本身。

诸多对《形而上学》的导读包括：英国学者乔纳森·巴恩斯的《剑桥亚里士多德导读》[6]、约翰·安克利尔的《哲学家亚里士多德》[7]、迈克尔·路克斯的《基本的"第一本体"：亚里士多德〈形而上学〉卷 7 和卷 8 解读》。[8] 学者们寻求对《形而上学》中的观点最精确的解释，力图揭示亚里士多德的原意。这一路径不仅涉及观点的阐释，还涉及对写作该书时周遭环境的研究。例如，学者们通常认为《形而上学》由亚里士多德自己撰写；但究竟是亚里士多德还是后来的编辑者把它编排为现有顺序，这个问题至今仍有争议。但巴恩斯等具有历史性思维的阐释者，主要关注《形而上学》本身该如何被理解的问题。

1. 大卫·塞德利:"古代哲学",载《简明劳德里奇哲学百科全书》,爱德华·克雷格编,伦敦:劳德里奇出版社,2005年,第17页。
2. 萨贾德·里兹维:"阿维森纳(伊本·西拿)",因特网哲学百科,登录日期2015年2月11日,http://www.iep.utm.edu/avicenna/。
3. 诺尔曼·克雷茨曼和艾兰诺·斯顿普,"托马斯·阿奎那",载《简明劳德里奇哲学百科全书》,爱德华·克雷格编,伦敦:劳德里奇出版社,2005年,第36页。
4. 保罗·托姆:"逻辑形式",载《中世纪哲学手册》,约翰·马仁邦编,牛津:牛津大学出版社,2013年,第273页。
5. 特伦斯·欧文:"亚里士多德",载《简明劳德里奇哲学百科全书》,爱德华·克雷格编,伦敦:劳德里奇出版社,2005年,第67页。
6. 乔纳森·巴恩斯编:《剑桥亚里士多德导读》,剑桥:剑桥大学出版社,1995年。
7. J. L. 安克利尔:《哲学家亚里士多德》,牛津:牛津大学出版社,1981年。
8. 迈克尔·路克斯:《基本的"第一本体":亚里士多德〈形而上学〉卷7和卷8解读》,纽约州伊萨卡:康奈尔大学出版社,1991年。

11 当代印迹

要点

- 今天,《形而上学》被视为形而上学领域的经典著作。
- 名为本质主义*的哲学立场源自亚里士多德的著作,在过去几百年间它时而被批评,时而被捍卫。
- 20 世纪后半叶对形而上学兴趣的复兴,使得更多当代哲学家转向亚里士多德,寻求思想和灵感。

地位

亚里士多德的《形而上学》被公认为哲学史上、尤其是以它命名的哲学学科中最重要的著作之一,在成书约两千年后的今天,它仍然非常重要。

当代哲学家也发现,亚里士多德的某些论证足够充分,可以用来启发灵感。在某些情况下,亚里士多德思想甚至被当作一个发展新思想的平台。这两个因素的结合使得亚里士多德"……位于有史以来最伟大的哲学家之列。仅从哲学影响来判断的话,只有柏拉图能与他匹敌。亚里士多德的著作形塑了从古代晚期到文艺复兴时期多个世纪的哲学。即使今天,仍有人带着敏锐的、毫不古旧的兴趣研究他。"[1]

审视亚里士多德对当代辩论的影响,哲学家可被划归入两个阵营。一方面,哲学家不再看重亚里士多德在《形而上学》中探索的本体等中心议题;另一方面,20 世纪下半叶有一个对形而上学兴趣的复兴。结果是,当代形而上学家们转向亚里士多德的思想,寻求灵感和参照。古典主义者兼哲学家约翰·安克利尔认为："自那以后出版的许多书籍和文章中的话题都来自亚里士多德。事物和质量、物质和变化、可数名词和集体名词、主语和谓语，这些话题处于亚里士多德探索的中心，他对它们的处理，有着与现今形而上学家一样的对语言的强调和敏感。"2

> 亚里士多德位于有史以来最伟大的哲学家之列。仅从哲学影响来判断的话，只有柏拉图能与他匹敌。亚里士多德的著作形塑了从古代晚期到文艺复兴时期多个世纪的哲学。即使今天，仍有人带着敏锐的、毫不古旧的兴趣研究他……他现存的著作涉及众多学科，从逻辑学、形而上学、心灵哲学到伦理学……在所有这些领域，亚里士多德的理论都给予启发、遭到反对、引发争论，并一般都会激励并维系一个稳定读者群的兴趣。
> —— 克里斯托弗·希尔兹："亚里士多德"，《斯坦福哲学百科》

互动

亚里士多德《形而上学》中的观点仍旧挑战和影响着当代哲学辩论，但今天的哲学家很少直接使用亚里士多德的论证。亚氏讨论哲学问题的方式与现代哲学家提问的方式截然不同。如今流行的一些观念、理论假设，甚至哲学方法，都无法在亚里士多德的著作中找到；然而哲学家们仍旧以散漫的、诠释性的方式接近亚里士多德，从诸如《形而上学》等一些作品中汲取有用的、激发灵感的内容。例如，亚里士多德对本质属性和偶然属性的区别启发了现代本质主义理论。该理论认为任何事物都有一定的核心属性，用以构成它的身份和功能。

本质主义挑战了束理论等流行观点，该理论由苏格兰启蒙运动*哲学家大卫·休谟于 18 世纪提出。它认为对象是它们属性的总和，在形成一个对象的身份时，并不存在像本体或本质属性这样额外的实体。³ 新近对本质主义和亚里士多德本体思想兴趣的复兴显示出，尽管束理论流行过几个世纪，当代哲学家仍可通过适应当代形而上学语境的方式重新诠释古代思想（如亚里士多德的思想），向束理论提出挑战。

持续争议

1973 年，美国生物伦理学家巴鲁克·布洛迪*发表了一篇文章，名为《为什么不安然接受老式的亚里士多德本质主义呢？》。该文作者所维护的观点是，偶然属性和本质属性之间有区别，这与亚里士多德的本体观点相类似。在布洛迪看来，亚里士多德正确认识到，从某种意义上说，一些必不可少的属性构成了事物（比如人）的本质。布洛迪运用当代分析哲学*的工具，展示出松散地继承自亚里士多德《形而上学》中的本质属性思想的优势。与之类似，美国哲学家乔舒亚·霍夫曼*和加里·罗森克兰茨*也都支持本体概念。他们从研究亚里士多德的本体概念开始，最终批评它对于当代形而上学来说缺乏足够的细节；但显然亚氏的思想启发了他们的论述。⁴

本质主义的支持者仍是少数，但哲学家们也认识到，在关于属性的性质和身份的形而上学辩论方面，这些少数派做出了重要贡献。通过对《形而上学》的广泛诠释，现代哲学家都能够在当代思想中运用其中的观点。如此一来，直到今天，无论是作为一部塑造形而上学领域的著作，还是作为一个有趣又有说服力的思想源泉，《形而上学》都非常重要。

1. 克里斯托弗·希尔兹:"亚里士多德",《斯坦福哲学百科》,登录日期 2015 年 2 月 10 日,http://plato.stanford.edu/entries/aristotle/。
2. J. L. 安克利尔:《哲学家亚里士多德》,牛津:牛津大学出版社,1981 年,第 8 页。
3. 参见,例如,大卫·休谟:《人性论》1.4.6.3。
4. 乔舒亚·霍夫曼和加里·S. 罗森克兰茨:《本体的本质与存在》,伦敦和纽约:劳德里奇出版社,1997 年。

12 未来展望

要 点

- 《形而上学》很可能一直是形而上学领域的一部关键性著作。
- 它的历史价值和哲学价值都将得到研究。
- 无论对形而上学这一具体学科,还是对更普遍的哲学辩论,该书都产生了深远影响,鲜有其他著作能够企及。

潜力

亚里士多德的《形而上学》自完成以来就在哲学讨论中发挥着重要作用:对哲学家和其他思想家来说,它仍是一部非常重要的著作。

在古代世界以及中世纪的西方和伊斯兰教哲学中,《形而上学》都对与它同名的哲学分支的发展产生了重要影响。这些传统中的大多数(如果不是全部的话)哲学家都从亚里士多德著作中获益或受其启发。如英国哲学家乔纳森·巴恩斯所说:"对亚里士多德知识遗产的盘点,不会比整个欧洲思想史少多少"。[1]

如今我们似乎处在一个更普遍的对亚里士多德哲学兴趣的复兴之中。美国哲学家爱德华·费瑟*评论道:"如果说亚里士多德主义正处于全面复兴状态,肯定会有些夸大其词。但一些相关的各式各样的思想流派至少正开始汇聚起来,成为某种自觉的思想运动。"[2]

《形而上学》因其哲学内容始终处于学术关注的中心。与对之前时代的影响力相比,该文本如今的影响力要小一些。当代哲学家通常认为亚里士多德关于本体的主要论点略微过时了。

由于当代关注不同于古代,受亚里士多德形而上学学说启发的当代思想家都不会特别运用他的确切论证。与之相反,他们运用亚氏引入的概念,如本质的概念、存在、形式质料说、潜在和实在。当代哲学家重新诠释这些观点,并吸收进对当代问题的讨论中。有鉴于亚里士多德这本《形而上学》的宏大和复杂,未来哲学家很可能继续在它的字里行间寻找灵感。

> 对亚里士多德知识遗产的盘点,不会比整个欧洲思想史少多少。
>
> —— 乔纳森·巴恩斯:《简明亚里士多德导读》

未来方向

亚里士多德的《形而上学》仍是哲学家、哲学史家和知识分子必不可少的阅读对象。出于注疏原因对《形而上学》感兴趣的思想家,试图通过某种方式揭示亚里士多德的原意。他们都相信,无论对形而上学的发展,还是作为一部哲学著作本身,该书都有着重要地位。这一路径不仅涉及对亚氏观点的诠释,还涉及对文本撰写时环境的探索。学者们一致同意《形而上学》由亚里士多德本人撰写,但究竟是亚氏还是后来的编辑者把书中章节编排为现有顺序,他们意见还不统一。

相比之下,具有历史思维的诠释者通常关注的问题是,我们该如何理解《形而上学》。关于这一路径的最好例子可以在各种研究和评论中找到,例如,乔纳森·比尔的《行与是:亚里士多德〈形而上学〉卷9解析》[3],或哲学家大卫·博斯托克对《形而上学》

卷 7 和卷 8 的翻译与评论。⁴

其他当代思想家将《形而上学》中的观点用作他们自己理论的灵感。这些学者通常都不特别关注亚里士多德的原意，而是评估和辩论亚氏思想的哲学性。例如，近些年美国哲学家乔舒亚·霍夫曼和加里·罗森克兰茨认为，本体概念尤其是亚里士多德对本质属性和偶然属性的区分，不仅在哲学上是有趣的，而且与反对本体存在的形而上学论述比起来，它也是更受欢迎的。⁵ 讨论过亚氏的观点之后，霍夫曼和罗森克兰茨提出他们自己的观点，这些观点受到亚氏对本体论述的影响。

当代芬兰哲学家图奥马斯·塔科*也对亚里士多德《形而上学》有着持久的兴趣。在最新著作中，他认为，思考当代形而上学的范围时，可以将亚里士多德的形而上学概念视为"第一哲学"。⁶

这些现代著作表明，在撰写完成两千年后的今天，《形而上学》仍对哲学有着重大意义。

小结

在近两千年来哲学思想的发展中，亚里士多德的《形而上学》始终居于核心地位。如今的学者阅读和讨论这部开创性著作，不仅因为它在哲学史上的重要作用，还因为它所提出的观点在哲学辩论中不断涌现。即使当今的思想家们，也能从亚里士多德古老的概念和论述中找到灵感。

亚里士多德的《形而上学》是一部独特的著作，它融合了敏锐的哲学思想和严谨的哲学论证。它比其他任何存世的古代著作都更大地影响了形而上学的发展。由于吸引了一大批来自不同文化背景和历史时期的思想家，亚氏的这个文本可能一直具有重要性。他的诸如"存在之存在"、本体、形式质料说、潜在与实在等概念，直至今天仍持续不断进入哲学辩论中。哲学史学家分析这些普遍意义上重要的形而上学观点，以更好地理解它们的含义；实践哲学家重新发现它们，通过在前沿讨论中运用它们以赋予其新的生命。讨论的深刻性和观点的复杂性都表明，亚里士多德的《形而上学》仍有潜力与未来可能广泛的大范围的哲学辩论相关联。

---

1. 乔纳森·巴恩斯：《简明亚里士多德导读》，牛津：牛津大学出版社，2000年，第136页。
2. 爱德华·费瑟："引言：一场亚里士多德复兴？"载《亚里士多德的方法与形而上学》，爱德华·费瑟编，纽约：帕尔格雷夫－麦克米伦出版社，2013年，第2页。
3. 乔纳森·比尔：《行与是：亚里士多德〈形而上学〉卷9解析》，牛津：牛津大学出版社，2009年。
4. 亚里士多德：《〈形而上学〉卷7与卷8》，大卫·博斯托克译注，牛津：克拉伦登出版社，1994年。
5. 乔舒亚·霍夫曼和加里·S.罗森克兰茨：《本体的本质与存在》，伦敦和纽约：劳德里奇出版社，1997年。
6. 图奥马斯·塔科："作为第一哲学的形而上学"，载《亚里士多德的方法与形而上学》，爱德华·费瑟编，纽约：帕尔格雷夫－麦克米伦出版社，2013年，第49—67页。

术语表

1. **阿加德米学园**：公元前 4 世纪，亚里士多德的老师柏拉图创建的哲学学校。

2. **偶然属性**：定义某个对象的非必要属性。例如，翘鼻子是人的偶然属性，因为鼻子的形状因人而异，它不是所有人都具备的某种根本属性。

3. **实在**：见潜在和实在。

4. **分析哲学**：当代哲学的分支。从广义上讲，分析哲学家的研究方法不同于其他哲学家，前者的研究基于逻辑和严谨的分析。

5. **古代**：在中世纪之前、西方人类史之内的一段时期。

6. **阿派朗**：由前苏格拉底派哲学家阿那克西曼德引入的一个哲学概念，字面义为"无限"。它表示存在一种根本的创造原则，有着特定的生成属性，不同于任何常见元素的属性。

7. **雅典**：亚里士多德时代希腊哲学学习的中心。它是世界上最古老的城市之一，至少 7 000 年前就有人居住。

8. **存在之存在**：亚里士多德引入的一个短语，对其最佳的理解是"作为存在的存在"。亚氏借它来描述自己对存在的探寻，也即对我们今天所谓的本体论的探寻。

9. **束理论**：一个形而上学理论，认为对象可以理解为它们所拥有的所有属性的集合或"束"。有观点认为对象有着决定它们身份特殊性的本质属性，束理论是此观点的替代项。

10. **基督徒**：根据耶稣·基督的教义信奉基督教的人。

11. **古典希腊**：从公元前 5 世纪到公元前 4 世纪，持续约两百年的希腊文化时期。

12. **宇宙学**：将宇宙作为整体的研究。在古代哲学语境中，它指世界的起源、活跃的世界原动力等问题。

13. **近代早期**：从中世纪晚期开始的一段历史时期，大约从公元 1500 年至 1800 年。

14. **经验主义**：相信知识是在体验和观察的基础上获得的。

15. **启蒙运动**：18 世纪的智识运动，以强调理性、反对传统为标志。

16. **本质主义**：认为对象具有某些构成它们身份的核心属性或特征。

17. **注疏**：对文本的批判性分析和解读。

18. **希腊化时期**：亚历山大大帝死亡至古罗马帝国崛起之间的 3 个世纪，一般认为是公元前 323 年至公元前 31 年。

19. **形式质料说**：该思想认为本体是事物中显现的形式，它最早由亚里士多德提出。

20. **固有形式**：在事物中显现的形式，不同于独立存在的形式。亚里士多德第一个提出包含该概念的理论。

21. **无形的**：形容词，用来描述没有物理实体的对象。

22. **伊斯兰教**：一种宗教，它的信徒视安拉为唯一的神，信奉先知穆罕默德。

23. **逻各斯**：在古代哲学家中非常流行、同时又出名地难译的一个概念，专指人或世界本身的合理性。它在希腊前苏格拉底派哲学家赫拉克利特的思想中有着重要作用，该哲学家认为逻各斯是构成世界的原理。

24. **吕克昂学园**：公元前 4 世纪，亚里士多德在雅典创建的哲学学校，其中的学员被称为逍遥派。

25. **马其顿**：古典希腊北部边缘的一个王国，是亚里士多德和亚历山大大帝的出生地，后者后来成为该王国的国王。

26. **中世纪时期**：又称中世纪，欧洲历史中从公元 5 世纪至公元 15 世纪的一段时期。

27. **形而上学**：哲学的子领域，处理与生存、现实或存在本身相关的问题。

28. **客籍民**：该词用来描述一个人的社会和政治地位，他居住在古雅典，但却并非全权公民。与全权公民不同，客籍民只能部分地参与政治生活，无法拥有土地，还要缴纳额外的税金。

29. **中世纪**：从公元 5 世纪至公元 15 世纪的欧洲历史时期。

30. **米利都学派**：最早的希腊思想流派，以它所处的城镇（米利都）命名。其中最著名的成员包括：泰勒斯、阿那克西曼德、阿那克西美尼。

31. **新柏拉图主义者**：由普罗提诺创建的新柏拉图学派的成员。

32. **本体论**：形而上学的子领域；它涉及与存在相关的问题，如"世界上存在着什么？""存在都有什么类型？"和"该如何对存在归类？"等。

33. **参与**：一个标准的哲学术语，用来描述现实世界中的对象如何与形式相互作用。

34. **逍遥派**：亚里士多德的追随者。据说这个名字来源于希腊语单词"散步"，因为亚里士多德喜欢一边散步一边讲授他的课程。

35. **柏拉图式的**：与柏拉图相关的著作和思想。

36. **柏拉图主义**：柏拉图的哲学。

37. **潜在和实在**：亚里士多德提出的概念，指代对象的模态。潜在指以某种方式变化的可能性或能力。实在指变化的能力已完成的状态。

例如，一个橡子是潜在的橡树，而橡树则是实在的本体。

38. **前苏格拉底学派**：苏格拉底时代及之前时代（约公元前469年至公元前399年）一大批活跃的希腊哲学家。他们持各自不同的观点，有时被归为不同流派，但他们都对形而上学和自然科学感兴趣。

39. **文艺复兴**：该词本意为"重生"，指14至17世纪的一段历史时期，以欧洲艺术和文学的复兴为标志。

40. **罗马**：与古罗马文明有关，始于公元前8世纪的意大利半岛，持续至公元5世纪。在实力和影响力最为强劲的公元1世纪和2世纪，它扩张为占地650万平方公里（约250万平方英里）的帝国。

41. **斯多葛派**：一个古老的哲学流派，尤以其激进的伦理观点而闻名。他们也提出了一系列重要的形而上学和认识论思想。

42. **本体**：表示对象本质的一个哲学概念，它不同于对象所拥有的其他偶然属性。本体理论的支持者相信，一个人的本体，例如说，不同于他脸色苍白或有个翘鼻子。据亚里士多德所说，本体是一个固有的形式，它显现在物质中。

43. **本质属性**：定义对象的根本属性。人的根本属性应为所有人共享的、成为人所必需的。

44. **理式论**：该理论指出，每一类属性都有一种普遍的形式，一种永恒的、无形的、存在于实在世界之外的实体，它既是属性的完美例证，也是属性存在的原因。例如，人凭借"参与"人的形式，享有成为人共有的属性。

45. **第三人论证**：由亚里士多德提出的批评柏拉图理式论的一个论证。它表明，形式不可能是普遍的，因为它们自己的存在也需要一个普遍形式。

46. **普遍性**：指所有同类对象共有的共通特征。它的反面是特殊性，即一类中具体的个体。例如,你的宠物狗是普遍的"狗"中的一个特殊例子。

47. **不动的动者**:在亚里士多德看来,这个动者是宇宙中所有变化的第一原因。它引发运动,但它本身的运动却不由任何先在的动作所引发。亚氏思考过是否存在多个或一个不动的动者,但他的结论尚不清晰。

人名表

1. 约翰·安克利尔（1921—2007），英国古典主义者和哲学家。他在亚里士多德哲学上做出了几项重要研究。

2. 亚历山大大帝（公元前356—公元前323），马其顿国王，以发动过大规模的军事征服战争而闻名。在全盛时期，他的帝国从地中海东部地区延伸至喜马拉雅山脉。

3. 阿弗罗狄西亚的亚历山大，逍遥派评论家和哲学家，活跃于3世纪初，以评论亚里士多德的各类作品而闻名。

4. 阿那克西曼德（约公元前610—约公元前546），前苏格拉底派中米利都学派的一员，因引入阿派朗（"无限"）理论而闻名。该理论认为，世界由一种不同于任何普通元素的类元素物所生成。

5. 阿那克西美尼（约公元前585—约公元前528），前苏格拉底派中米利都学派的一员。他最著名的论点为气是世界的基本原理和构成材料。

6. 罗得岛的安德罗尼柯，一位逍遥派哲学家，因在公元前1世纪时编辑并出版亚里士多德的著作而闻名。对他本人人们所知甚少，仅有他自己著作的零星片段留存。

7. 托马斯·阿奎那（1225—1274），中世纪最著名的哲学家兼神学家之一。在哲学的大部分领域，从形而上学到伦理学，他都撰写过作品，其中最著名的是《神学大全》和《反异教大全》。

8. 阿威罗伊（伊本·路西德）（1126—1198），伊斯兰哲学家，尤其以对亚里士多德的评论而著名。

9. 阿维森纳（伊本·西拿）（980—1037），波斯哲学家和知识分子，尤以对医学发展做出的贡献而著名。他的哲学著作内容充实，其中关于存在的本体论理论受亚里士多德影响很大。

10. 乔纳森·巴恩斯（1942年生），牛津大学哲学专业荣休教授，当代最著名的古代哲学专家之一，出版过多部关于古代哲学家的作品。

11. **乔纳森·比尔**，柏林洪堡大学古代哲学和科学史专业教授。他的研究领域为古代哲学，已出版多部有关亚里士多德《形而上学》的著作。

12. **大卫·博斯托克**（1936年生），牛津大学哲学专业荣休教授，已出版多部有关古代哲学尤其是柏拉图和亚里士多德的著作。

13. **巴鲁克·布洛迪**（1943年生），田纳西州莱斯大学哲学教授，他以伦理学尤其是生物医学、伦理学著作而闻名。

14. **托马斯·凯斯**（1844—1925），牛津大学道德哲学和形而上学哲学教授。他以当代形而上学著作而出名，也出版过几部关于亚里士多德的作品。

15. **S. 马克·科恩**，华盛顿大学哲学专业荣休教授。他是古代哲学专家，已出版多部有关亚里士多德的著作。

16. **德摩斯梯尼**（公元前384—公元前322），古雅典雄辩家和政治家，尤以其政治演讲而闻名。

17. **恩培多克勒**（公元前490—公元前430），前苏格拉底派哲学家，多个著名学说的作者。他因最先提出四元素理论（火、水、土、气）而闻名。

18. **爱德华·费瑟**（1968年生），加州帕萨迪纳市帕萨迪纳城市学院哲学副教授，已出版一系列有关历史哲学和当代哲学的著作。

19. **劳埃德·格尔森**，多伦多大学哲学教授，知名古代哲学研究专家，已出版许多涉及不同主题的著作。

20. **义赛托特·哈多特**，法国国立科学研究中心荣休教授。她出版过多部有关古代哲学，尤其是新柏拉图主义的著作。

21. **维里蒂·哈特**，耶鲁大学哲学与古典文学专业教授，她擅长古代哲学，尤为关注柏拉图和亚里士多德。

22. **赫拉克利特**（公元前535—公元前475），最著名的前苏格拉底派哲学

家之一。他认为掌管世界的是逻各斯，一种他比作火的理性。

23. **乔舒亚·霍夫曼**，北卡罗来纳大学格林斯博罗分校哲学教授，以他关于形而上学和神学的著作而闻名。

24. **大卫·休谟**（1711—1776），重要的苏格兰哲学家，尤其以他的哲学经验主义而闻名，该理论的主要信条是知识的主要来源是感觉。

25. **特伦斯·欧文**（1947年生），牛津大学古代哲学教授，古代哲学和伦理学史方面的专家。

26. **安东尼·肯尼**（1931年生），牛津大学哲学专业荣休教授，著名古代哲学和亚里士多德研究专家。

27. **克劳德·帕纳乔**（1946年生），魁北克大学哲学教授，中世纪哲学专家。

28. **巴门尼德**（公元前6世纪末或公元前5世纪初），前苏格拉底派哲学家，爱利亚哲学学派创始人，以他在残篇诗歌《论自然》中提出的关于现实的矛盾性理论而著名。

29. **柏拉图**（公元前429—公元前347），希腊哲学家，哲学史上最重要的人物之一。他最著名的作品包括对话体的《理想国》《蒂迈欧篇》和《申辩篇》。

30. **普罗提诺**（204—270），新柏拉图主义哲学流派的奠基人，在作品《九章集》中，他创造出一个复杂而缜密的哲学体系。

31. **加里·罗森克兰茨**，北卡罗来纳大学格林斯博罗分校哲学教授，因在形而上学和神学问题上的著作而出名。

32. **西奥多·斯堪瑟斯**（1949年生），爱丁堡大学哲学教授，研究领域为古代哲学和当代形而上学。

33. **大卫·塞德利**（1947年生），剑桥大学古代哲学教授，古代哲学多个领域的知名学者。

34. **罗伯特·沙普尔斯**（1949—2010），职业生涯中很长一段时期，他都是伦敦大学学院希腊语与拉丁语系教授，他因在古希腊哲学方面的著作而受人尊敬。

35. 克里斯托弗·希尔兹，圣母大学哲学教授，古代哲学专家，写过不少有关亚里士多德的著作。

36. 苏格拉底（公元前470或469—公元前399），希腊哲学家，西方哲学传统中最重要的人物之一，因其严谨的哲学提问方式和对伦理问题的兴趣而闻名。他未留下文字作品，我们对他的了解都来自他的学生尤其是柏拉图的作品。

37. 图奥马斯·塔科，赫尔辛基大学哲学专业副教授，主攻当代形而上学。

38. 泰勒斯（约公元前624—公元前546），前苏格拉底时代米利都学派的成员之一，通常被认为是希腊传统中第一位哲学家。他最著名的观点是水是构成世界基本的原理和材料。

WAYS IN TO THE TEXT

KEY POINTS

- Born in 384 B.C.E., Aristotle spent most of his life in Athens, * Greece, where he studied with Plato, * established his own school, and wrote his works. He died in 322 B.C.E.

- *Metaphysics* challenged long-established philosophical theories about the nature of being, including those of Aristotle's teacher, Plato.

- Much of the history of philosophy has involved debate about the relative merits of Plato's and Aristotle's theories. While neither can claim absolute relevance today, Aristotle's work still provides intellectual food for thought for new generations of philosophers.

Who Was Aristotle?

Born in the Greek city of Stageira in 384 B.C.E., Aristotle became one of the most important teachers and philosophers of the ancient world. His father, a court doctor in Macedonia* (on the northern edges of Classical Greece), taught him biology and empirical* studies, that is the means of gaining knowledge based on observation or experience. At the age of 17, Aristotle moved to Athens and joined the Academy, * the school founded by the renowned philosopher Plato. He studied there until Plato's death in 347 B.C.E. Plato had himself studied with the great philosopher Socrates, * which gave Aristotle access to the prime philosophical wisdom of the era.

After Plato died, Aristotle returned to the Macedonian court and became the tutor of a nine-year-old boy named Alexander. The child would grow up to become one of the most powerful rulers of the ancient world: Alexander the Great.* Aristotle tutored

Alexander until the boy turned 16. In 335 B.C.E., Aristotle returned to Athens and established his own school, the Lyceum.* He wrote most of his key works—including *Metaphysics*—while he was there. He left Athens again in 322 B.C.E. and died later that year.

Unfortunately, very little of Aristotle's work survives. In fact, his reputation faded not long after his death and it was not until around three centuries later, when a Roman editor named Andronicus* collected and published Aristotle's essays, that his work became central to the study of philosophy. The book's title, *Metaphysics*, even gave a name to the philosophical discipline dedicated to studying the fundamental nature of being. But Aristotle died long before his editor coined the word metaphysics, * and the editor may have meant it to signify nothing more than the book's placement in Aristotle's body of work—that it came after (the Greek word *meta*) his work entitled *Physics*.

What Does *Metaphysics* Say?

For centuries before Aristotle, thinkers pursuing ontology*—the study of the nature of being—had theorized about what "being" actually is. Earlier philosophers had suggested that "substance"*—the thing that underlies all existence—was the air. Another thought it was water. A third thought fire. Yet another decided substance was, in fact, a combination of four elements, adding "earth" to the mix. Then in the fourth century B.C.E., Aristotle's teacher Plato changed the discussion forever when he theorized that eternal, bodiless "forms" existing independently in the world create the realities we perceive. This became known as Plato's Theory of Forms.*

Despite the fact that he had studied with Plato, Aristotle did not hesitate to disagree with his teacher's conclusions. Abandoning the notion of bodiless (or incorporeal)* forms, Aristotle suggested that form only exists when it is present in matter. He pointed out a logical inconsistency in Plato's theory. If every object requires a form to copy so that it may come into existence, then a man must have a "form" of a man to copy. And where does that form come from? This has become known as the "third man"* argument.

Aristotle primarily aims to investigate what he calls "being qua being"*—"qua" meaning "by virtue of what is." But in the loose collection of ideas that make up *Metaphysics*, other subjects arise as well. Aristotle also tackles concepts such as "potentiality" and "actuality,"* using them to answer a philosophical question that the philosopher Parmenides* had raised over a century earlier. Essentially, Parmenides' complex argument made the case that because there is no such thing as a state of non-being, change is essentially impossible. Aristotle disagreed with that argument by making a distinction between being-as-potential and being-as-actuality. A child exists both as a potential adult and as an actual child. In Aristotle's view, change did not involve the transformation from a state of non-being to being but from a state of potentiality into one of actuality.

Another important argument Aristotle developed in *Metaphysics* is the theory of the "unmoved mover"*—a kind of heavenly catalyst that serves as the source of all movement in the world. Are there many unmoved movers or only one? Aristotle's conclusions remain unclear, as he makes a case for each idea in different books in *Metaphysics*.

Supporting his theories through his strong analytical skills and powers of observation, Aristotle accepted some previous scholarship while overturning long-held beliefs about the nature of existence. He also raised a host of new questions for future philosophers to deal with—part of the reason his work remained central to the discipline of philosophy for so long. Subsequent generations of philosophers would continue to debate the merits of Platonic* versus Aristotelian interpretations. In some ways, the debates inspired by Aristotle's thought continue today and Aristotle's reputation as one of the founding minds of philosophy remains unquestioned.

Why Does *Metaphysics* Matter?

In *Metaphysics*, Aristotle tackled a subject that philosophers had been debating for centuries before him: what is "being"? While that question remains central to the study of metaphysics, the answers Aristotle offered nearly two thousand years ago continue to be relevant to the discussion.

While a number of Aristotle's works have survived, even if he had written nothing but *Metaphysics* his reputation would be assured. His work has influenced philosophers throughout the centuries—from the ancient Greeks of his day to the Romans, * to medieval* philosophers in Christian* and Islamic* cultures, all the way to the present day. Twelfth-century Islamic philosopher Averroes (Ibn Rushd)* and Christian cleric Thomas Aquinas* in the thirteenth century both used Aristotelian concepts in their work. In the eighteenth century, Scottish philosopher David Hume*—whose philosophy held, in essence, that one cannot know anything for certain without evidence—criticized Aristotle for having drawn unsupported conclusions about substance. After Hume, Aristotle's influence began to decline. But nevertheless, his works remained a part of the academic curriculum, as they do today.

In the second half of the twentieth century, philosophers revived their interest in metaphysics. The concerns metaphysicians address today differ from those considered in Aristotle's time, but scholars still recognize the historical and philosophical importance of his work. Some study *Metaphysics* and his other works exegetically*— that is, analyzing and interpreting the text to try to get to Aristotle's original meaning. Others look to this ancient text as a source of fresh inspiration. These scholars adapt Aristotle's thinking to the present day and seek to expand on his insights. For instance, Aristotle's ideas about the difference between substantial properties* and accidental properties* has inspired the modern theory of essentialism.* Essentialism holds that every entity has certain core attributes that constitute its identity and function. As the essentialist theory challenges Hume, in a sense we have come full circle. Hume refuted Aristotle; Aristotelian thinking refutes Hume.

British philosopher Jonathan Barnes* noted that "an account of Aristotle's intellectual afterlife would be little less than a history of European thought."[1] As we seem to be in the midst of a revival of interest in Aristotle's work today, that afterlife continues.

---

[1] Jonathan Barnes, *A Very Short Introduction to Aristotle* (Oxford: Oxford University Press, 2000), 136.

SECTION 1
INFLUENCES

MODULE 1
THE AUTHOR AND THE HISTORICAL CONTEXT

KEY POINTS

- *Metaphysics* is one of the most important works in the history of its philosophical discipline.
- The time Aristotle spent in Athens* among other philosophers greatly influenced his work.
- Plato's* mentorship was especially important for the development of Aristotle's thought.

Why Read This Text?

One of the most important works of ancient philosophy, Aristotle's *Metaphysics* consists of 14 treatises, named after letters of the Greek alphabet, which address various metaphysical topics. In fact, the name of the philosophical subfield of metaphysics* comes from the title of this book.

Metaphysics asks the central question: what is substance?* As philosophy professor Christopher Shields* explains, in this work Aristotle argues that, "it is ... possible to study all beings insofar as they are related to the core instance of being, and then also to study that core instance, namely substance."[1] Aristotle most prominently addresses the question of substance in book Zeta of *Metaphysics*. The other books contain discussions more or less pertinent to this topic as well, but they focus mostly on other issues. Examples of this are as follows:

- The explanation and assessment of philosophical thinking

in the time before the Greek philosopher Socrates* (an era known as pre-Socratic).*
- A critique of the philosopher Plato's Theory of Forms*—that non-material forms or ideas rather than the material world we know through our sensations are most fundamentally real.
- Relationships between parts and wholes—the study of parts and wholes concerns such questions as whether there are composite objects (complex objects with sub-parts) whose existence consists of more than *just* the sum of their parts.

Among the more famous ideas Aristotle presents in *Metaphysics* are the discussion of the nature of change and the idea that the first cause of all change in the universe is an unmoved mover.* This unmoved mover moves other things, but is not itself moved by any previous action.

Aristotle's analysis of these topics greatly influenced the debates on metaphysics in antiquity* (the period before the Middle Ages,* but within the span of Western human history), the Middle Ages, and beyond, even to the present day. Anyone who wishes to study the history of philosophical thought or to investigate central metaphysical questions more generally would do well to begin with *Metaphysics*.

> "Aristotle was born, 15 years after Socrates' death, in the small colony of Stagira, on the peninsula of Chalcidice. He was the son of Nicomachus, court physician to King Amyntas, the grandfather of Alexander the Great. After the death of his father he migrated to Athens in 367, being then 17, and joined Plato's Academy. He remained for 20 years

> as Plato's pupil and colleague, and it can safely be said that on no other occasion in history was such intellectual power concentrated in a single institution."
>
> —— Anthony Kenny, *Ancient Philosophy: A New History of Western Philosophy*

Author's Life

Born in 384 B.C.E. in the Greek city of Stageira, Aristotle learned biology and empirical* studies (gaining knowledge based on experience or observation) from his father, a court doctor in Macedonia.* The most important stage in Aristotle's education, however, came when he moved to Athens and joined Plato's school, the Academy, * in 367 B.C.E. He remained there until Plato's death in 347 B.C.E.

After leaving the Academy, Aristotle tutored future king and warrior Alexander the Great* in Macedonia. Returning to Athens in 335 B.C.E., he established the Lyceum, * his own philosophical school, and here he wrote all his major works, including *Metaphysics*. "This second period of residency in Athens was an astonishingly productive one for Aristotle ... many of the philosophical works of Aristotle that we possess today probably derive from this period."[2]

As with most ancient philosophers, we know little about the details of Aristotle's life. But the rich intellectual culture of Athens surely played a key role in the development of his thought.

Athens was a significant political center. Aristotle would have been able to develop his political thoughts by watching politics firsthand. As for the study of metaphysics, Athens provided an environment in which a thinker such as Aristotle would not just be introduced to a variety of philosophical concepts, but would also observe these ideas being put to the test through philosophical debates. His education therefore meant that he became well acquainted with the ideas that he later criticized and rejected in *Metaphysics*. The most important of these was Plato's Theory of Forms.

Author's Background

Despite being a well-known member of the philosophical community, Aristotle had limited social status, because he was not a full citizen of Athens. As a resident alien—a "metic"* in Greek—he could not fully participate in the political life of Athens, could not own land, and had to pay higher taxes than a full citizen. We can only speculate on this, but it might have been his metic status that led him to leave Athens after Plato's death. Scholar Jonathan Barnes* describes one possible scenario: "In 347 the northern town of Olynthus has just fallen to the Macedonian army, and the anti-Macedonian party in Athens, led by the orator Demosthenes, * was in the ascendant. Aristotle was not—then or ever—an Athenian citizen, and this situation may have been delicate."[3] The reappearance of anti-Macedonian feeling 25 years later caused him to leave Athens again at the very end of his life.[4]

Although the restrictions placed on a resident alien must have affected Aristotle in some way, his work does not reflect this. His intellectual surroundings were exceptionally favorable for philosophical activities. Aristotle spent 20 years in Plato's Academy and Plato was himself a pupil of Socrates. As philosophy professor Anthony Kenny* notes, "... it can safely be said that on no other occasion in history was such intellectual power concentrated in a single institution."⁵

---

1. Christopher Shields, "Aristotle, " *Stanford Encyclopedia of Philosophy*, accessed February 10, 2015, http: //plato.stanford.edu/entries/aristotle/.
2. Christopher Shields, "Aristotle's Philosophical Life and Writing, " in *The Oxford Handbook of Aristotle*, ed. Christopher Shields (Oxford: Oxford University Press, 2012), 8.
3. Jonathan Barnes, "Life and work, " in *The Cambridge Companion to Aristotle*, ed. Jonathan Barnes (Cambridge: Cambridge University Press, 1995), 4–5.
4. Barnes, "Life and work, " 6.
5. Anthony Kenny, *Ancient Philosophy: A New History of Western Philosophy* (Oxford: Oxford University Press, 2006), 65.

MODULE 2
ACADEMIC CONTEXT

KEY POINTS
- The field of metaphysics* addresses the questions pertinent to existence and reality or, according to Aristotle's famous claim, "being qua being"*—being by virtue of being.
- Pre-Socratic* philosophers had all analyzed the topic of fundamental existence, as had Aristotle's teacher Plato.*
- Aristotle made significant contributions to the development of metaphysical tradition.

The Work in Its Context

Aristotle did not title his work *Metaphysics*. Some three centuries after his death, a Roman editor named Andronicus* collected the essays that make up the book and gave them this title. Why? A common explanation is that Andronicus intended to show that this work came after Aristotle's writing on physics. The literal meaning of the Greek phrase *meta ta physica* is "after the physics."

But thanks to Andronicus, the subfield of philosophy that Aristotle's work spawned has been named after it. Broadly speaking, the discipline of metaphysics addresses questions about existence, reality, or being itself. Aristotle wrote, "There is a science which investigates being as being ... Now this is not the same as any of the so-called special sciences; for none of these others deals generally with being as being."[1] Studying "being qua being" became a defining concept for metaphysics. It is best understood in this way: "The science is in some sense wholly general or universal, for it is contrasted with the special sciences, each of which 'cuts off' a portion of reality and studies it ... Our science, on the other hand, —or metaphysics ... —deals with beings in general."[2] Ever since Aristotle's time, metaphysics has referred to the study of problems concerning the fundamental existence or being, as opposed to studies dedicated to specific objects or phenomena.

> *"In searching for explanation, men inevitably encounter difficulties ... These difficulties are, for Aristotle, the starting point of philosophy. It is by working one's way through the puzzles or difficulties that philosophical wisdom grows. Hence Aristotle devotes an entire book of the* Metaphysics *simply to cataloguing the puzzles surrounding the question of what are the basic elements of reality."*
>
> ——Jonathan Lear, Aristotle: *The Desire to Understand*

Overview of the Field

Aristotle's *Metaphysics* defined its field in many ways. But it also has roots in previous philosophical tradition. As Aristotle himself notes in book Alpha of *Metaphysics*, many Greek philosophers before him engaged in the questions of ontology*—studying the nature of being. English philosopher Anthony Kenny* notes that, "most dissertations that begin with literature searches seek to show that all work hitherto has left a gap that will now be filled by the author's original research. Aristotle's *Metaphysics* is no exception ... The earliest philosophy, he concluded, is, on all subjects, full of babble, since in its beginnings it is but an infant."³

Most of the thinkers Aristotle counts as his predecessors were pre-Socratic philosophers. An especially important group of pre-Socratics was the Milesian* school, which took its name from Miletus, the town where it originated. As one introduction to ancient philosophy says, "The first pre-Socratics, Thales, * Anaximander, * and Anaximenes*— from Miletus in Asia Minor— were concerned to provide cosmologies, * reasoned accounts of the world we live in. As Aristotle acutely saw, they focused on what he called the material cause—the question of what our world is composed of."⁴

Aristotle found the scope of the ideas put forward by Milesians to be limited. But he did not always criticize them. He was positively impressed by other pre-Socratics such as Empedocles.* "Aristotle praised him for realizing that a cosmological theory must not just identify the elements of the universe, but must assign causes for the development and intermingling of the elements to make the living and inanimate compounds of the actual world."⁵ Pre-Socratic ideas, therefore, provided a rich intellectual soil in which Aristotle could develop his own views.

Academic Influences

Little evidence survives about Aristotle's intellectual life in general and the information we have can be contradictory. One of the questions on which sources disagree is the relationship between Aristotle and the previous intellectual tradition. One line of scholarship paints Aristotle as an especially arrogant person, condescending to both his contemporaries and earlier philosophers. The other line of scholarship says that Aristotle respected and cared about his friends and colleagues. Scholar Christopher Shields* concludes that, "we should simply admit what is plain: the negative remarks in the ancient biographical tradition surrounding Aristotle are mainly the views of his enemies, men driven by petty jealousy and competitive zeal rather than by a sober interest in neutral assessment."[6]

Aristotle's most important influence was probably his teacher Plato. Aristotle studied in Plato's Academy* for two decades, so it stands to reason that his intellectual relationship with the elder philosopher shaped his own development. That is not to say Aristotle embraced Plato's ideas wholeheartedly. Aristotle is known for criticizing Platonic* ideas. Although we cannot say exactly how Plato influenced Aristotle, it is clear that on the whole he was a positive influence.

Scholar Jonathan Barnes* argued that, "there are centrally Aristotelian texts for which Plato's views are evidently a main source of inspiration and of puzzlement (thus the last two books of the *Metaphysics* are largely moved by Platonic notions about mathematics) and—more vaguely but more importantly—whole areas of Aristotle's philosophical interests were shaped and determined by Plato's philosophical interests."[7]

---

1. Aristotle, *Metaphysics*, trans. William David Ross, in *The Complete Works of Aristotle: The Revised Oxford Translation*, ed. Jonathan Barnes (Princeton, NJ: Princeton University Press, 1984), 2: 1584.

2. Jonathan Barnes, "Metaphysics, " in *The Cambridge Companion to Aristotle*, ed. Jonathan Barnes (Cambridge: Cambridge University Press, 1995), 69.
3. Anthony Kenny, *Ancient Philosophy: A New History of Western Philosophy* (Oxford: Oxford University Press, 2006), 3.
4. Julia Annas, *Ancient Philosophy: A Very Short Introduction* (Oxford: Oxford University Press, 2000), 100.
5. Kenny, *Ancient Philosophy*, 22.
6. Christopher Shields, *Aristotle* (London: Routledge, 2007), 15.
7. Jonathan Barnes, "Life and work, " in *The Cambridge Companion to Aristotle*, ed. Jonathan Barnes (Cambridge: Cambridge University Press, 1995), 17–18.

MODULE 3
THE PROBLEM

KEY POINTS

- In the period when *Metaphysics* was conceived, philosophers generally engaged with questions relating to the fundamental principles of existence.
- A little before Aristotle's time, while his teacher Plato* was developing his Theory of Forms, * pre-Socratics* questioned the functioning of the natural world.
- Aristotle's work engages with the previous philosophical tradition both by using concepts created by earlier thinkers and by criticizing some of their views and approaches.

Core Question

Long before Aristotle wrote *Metaphysics*, one of the issues stirring heated debate among philosophers was the question of substance.* As Aristotle himself notes in book Zeta of *Metaphysics*, "the question which, both now and of old, has always been raised, and always been the subject of doubt, viz. what being is, is just the question, what is substance?"[1]

The philosophical notion of substance can be difficult to grasp as it has many nuances, but its core meaning remains relatively uncomplicated. We can best understand substances as "ontologically* basic entities: "[2] that is, a substance is the essence of an object, as opposed to any accidental properties* the object might have. For example, those who believe in substance theory say the substance of a person is distinct from physical attributes, such as being pale-skinned or having a snub nose. The notion of a substance depicts the very fundamental parts of an object's existence. Aristotle even claims that, "substance is a principle and a cause."[3]

The interest in fundamental existence goes back to the early pre-Socratic thinkers such as Thales,* Anaximander,* and Anaximenes.* They discussed the principles of how the world functions. Each of the pre-Socratics had a different idea about which natural element was responsible for the reality we experience. Thales, for instance, claimed that water is the primary principle underlying all existence. Anaximenes disagreed, arguing that it was air, while Anaximander proposed the existence of apeiron,* a special "limitless" element that generated the world. Later pre-Socratics continued this tradition. Heraclitus* argued that the world is governed by a principle based on rationality (logos),* which he also called fire. Empedocles,* meanwhile, was the first philosopher to introduce the theory of the four elements together (fire, water, earth, air).

Discussions about ontology—the study of the nature of being—changed dramatically in the Athens of the fourth century B.C.E., when Aristotle's teacher, Plato, introduced the notion of non-bodily forms as the causes of existence. In what are known as his middle dialogues, Plato presented the argument that incorporeal,* eternal, independently existing forms account for all reality. This theory turned out to be a game changer in metaphysical* debates in general, and an important innovation in debates on the nature of substance.

> "And indeed the question which, both now and of old, has always been raised, and always been the subject of doubt, viz. what being is, is just the question, what is substance?"
>
> ——Aristotle, *Metaphysics*

The Participants

Plato's metaphysics holds a very significant place in the history of philosophy in its own right. But it also provides an essential key to understanding Aristotle's position. Arguably Plato's most significant innovation was his Theory of Forms. This theory supposes that forms exist as causal entities.

In simpler terms, Plato's work makes a distinction between "being" and "becoming." While "becoming" describes the constantly changing, perishable, and unstable actual world, the forms—referred to as "being"—always stay the "same and in the same state."[4] The forms, moreover, act as causes of properties in the world of becoming. Plato saw objects in the world of becoming as partaking* in the forms. In this way, things in the actual world represent their respective forms, while at the same time, they are also "copies" or things derived from the forms. But forms are not derived from anything else. So Plato often states that only they—the forms—belong to the reality of true being.[5] A beautiful person, for instance, is beautiful by virtue of partaking in the form of beauty. This form constitutes what "beautiful" is, while the person is a kind of reflection of the form.

This complex theory has many implications. As British

philosopher and academic Verity Harte* explains, "Forms have a role to play in Plato's theory of being or what there is: 1. Forms are (among the primary) beings. 2. Further ... Forms are identified as having causal responsibility for things other than Forms having some of the character they do; the Form of beauty, for example, has causal responsibility for the beauty of anything else that is beautiful. In this way, Forms are not only themselves beings, they are causally responsible for at least certain other aspects of the character of the world, as well."[6] For this reason, "Forms are Plato's substances, for everything derives its existence from Forms."[7]

The Contemporary Debate

Aristotle criticizes Plato's ideas about substance throughout *Metaphysics*, and especially in books Zeta, Mu, and Nu. Aristotle's critique concentrates on Plato's idea that forms are both incorporeal (bodiless), eternal, independently existing entities and the causes of existence. According to Plato's view, an object becomes beautiful by partaking in the form of beauty, which represents perfect beauty and the origin of all the beauty in the world. This means that properties derive from forms. Aristotle saw things differently: "If, then, we view the matter from these standpoints, it is plain that no universal* attribute is a substance, and this is plain also from the fact that no common predicate indicates a 'this', but rather a 'such'. If not, many difficulties follow and especially the 'third man.'"[8] Aristotle's third man argument* contends that if Plato's forms cause existence, then these forms themselves need other forms in order to exist. For example, a man exists as a man by assuming the form of man. However, in order for this man's form to exist, there must be a form of a form of man—the third man—and so on.

Aristotle suggests that when discussing substances, we ought to be talking about objects themselves rather than their accidental properties. In his own theory, Aristotle discards the notion of incorporeal and eternal forms. He does use the notion of form, but in a rather different way from Plato. He writes, "by form I mean the essence of each thing and its primary substance."[9] Form, according to Aristotle, is immanent, * that is, it only exists when it is present in matter. But it is important to note the formulation. Substance is "form present in matter, " but not a *compound* of form and matter. Aristotle rejects the latter option, because compounds cannot be primary.[10] This philosophically rigorous and innovative idea made Aristotle one of the most important metaphysicians in the history of philosophy.

---

1 Aristotle, Metaphysics, trans. William David Ross, in *The Complete Works of Aristotle: The Revised Oxford Translation*, ed. Jonathan Barnes (Princeton, NJ: Princeton University Press, 1984), 2: 1624.

2. Michael J. Loux, *Primary "Ousia": An Essay on Aristotle's Metaphysics Z and H* (Ithaca, NY: Cornell University Press, 1991), 2.

3. Aristotle, *Metaphysics*, 2: 1644.

4. Plato, *Sophist*, trans. Nicholas P. White, in *Plato: Complete Works*, ed. John M. Cooper (Indianapolis, IN; Cambridge: Hackett Publishing Company, 1997), 269–70.

5. Plato, *Phaedo*, trans. G. M. A. Grube, in *Plato: Complete Works*, ed. John M. Cooper (Indianapolis, IN; Cambridge: Hackett Publishing Company, 1997), 86.

6. Verity Harte, "Plato's Metaphysics, " in *The Oxford Handbook of Plato*, ed. Gail Fine (Oxford:

Oxford University Press, 2008), 193–4.
7. Howard Robinson, "Substance, " *Stanford Encyclopedia of Philosophy*, accessed February 10, 2015, http: //plato.stanford.edu/entries/substance/.
8. Aristotle, *Metaphysics*, 2: 1640.
9. Aristotle, *Metaphysics*, 2: 1630.
10. Aristotle, *Metaphysics*, 2: 1625.

MODULE 4
THE AUTHOR'S CONTRIBUTION

KEY POINTS

- Aristotle criticizes Plato's* Theory of Forms* for considering substance* to be outside of, prior to, and more real than individual bodies. He argues that substance is an immanent* form—that is, a form present in matter.
- Aristotle's theory about substance challenges a common view of his day and raises a viable alternative that would become extremely influential among philosophers for many centuries.
- While Aristotle draws on some of Plato's theoretical assumptions, he provides a genuinely novel take on the pre-existing concepts.

Author's Aims

Aristotle claims in *Metaphysics* that he seeks the knowledge of "causes and principles."[1] In short, he dedicates this work to exploring the questions of the most fundamental ontology, * the study of the nature of being.

Arguably the most important topic he addresses in this work is his theory about substance. Scholars typically explain this theory as a response to Plato. But its importance mainly lies in Aristotle's substantial and well-argued account of substance, which scholars have recognized for centuries as a key contribution to metaphysics.* Although Aristotle may have felt he was simply adding to a well-developed debate, his contribution is an outstanding philosophical achievement in its own right. Aristotle's ideas challenged what had been widely accepted as a strong account of what substance is.

As professor of ancient philosophy, Theodore Scaltsas* explains, "Aristotle insists that the substantial form is not a further component part in a substance, but is of a different ontological type from the component parts. In doing so Aristotle is presenting us with his own theory, but at the same time he is offering a criticism of the Platonic* metaphysics."[2] In addition to showing that Plato's Theory of Forms had problematic aspects as an account of substance, Aristotle aimed to present a very different account of his own. Instead of placing substance in eternal, changeless, incorporeal objects outside of this world (as Plato had), Aristotle argued that substance is a form present in matter—an idea known as the immanence of form. Aristotle supported his argument with both strong analyses and astute observations.

> "All men suppose what is called wisdom to deal with the first causes and the principles of things. This is why, as has been said before, the man of experience is thought to be wiser than the possessors of any perception whatever, the artist wiser than the men of experience, the master-worker than the mechanic, and the theoretical kinds of knowledge to be more of the nature of wisdom than the productive. Clearly then wisdom is knowledge about certain causes and principles."
>
> —— Aristotle, *Metaphysics*

Approach

In his quest to define substance, Aristotle claims to be researching being. He notes that philosophers use the term "being" in a number of different ways, but then goes on to argue that primary being is the substance and then explains that when we talk about substantial being, we distinguish from merely accidental properties* as follows: "when we say of what quality a thing is, we say that it is good or beautiful, but not that it is three cubits long or that it is a man; but when we say what it is, we do not say 'white' or 'hot' or 'three cubits long', but 'man' or 'God.'"[3]

Although the underlying idea is similar to Plato's, Aristotle presents his investigation in a very different manner. Aristotle's thorough, methodical approach to answering very complex questions was unparalleled—both in the ancient world and afterwards. "*Metaphysics* ... uses Aristotle's most intricate and technical machinery in the service of some of the most demanding and fundamental problems in all of philosophy."[4]

Because Aristotle writes in a technical style and uses many extra concepts and side-investigations to support his search for a strong account of substance, *Metaphysics* remains a notoriously difficult text to read. Aristotle used a unique approach throughout his works. He organized his inquiry based on his idea that in order to investigate something, "one starts with what is familiar to us initially, and moves towards an understanding of first principles that are knowable by nature."[5]

Contribution in Context

Aristotle's account of substance is best understood in the context of his critique of Plato's Theory of Forms. Plato famously theorized about the existence of incorporeal universal* entities—forms—

as perfect examples of every existing object. Aristotle criticized Platonic forms, pointing out that the theory is susceptible to various objections, for instance the so-called third man argument.* Aristotle famously argued that if a man becomes a man by partaking* in the form of a man, then the form of a man also requires another form in order to be a form of a man, and so on.⁶

However, Aristotle also used the notion of "form" in his work. He argued that substance is an immanent form, that is, a form present in matter. Aristotle reinterpreted the received idea of the existence of forms and developed it into a distinct theory, "whereas for Plato it seemed vital to assert the existence of the forms apart and by themselves, at the same time as they in some mysterious way 'entered into' the concrete things which were called by their names, for Aristotle they were always in some physical body."⁷

As we can see from his engagement with Plato, Aristotle borrowed concepts from the tradition that already existed however, he also introduced genuinely novel interpretations of these ideas. Although Greek philosophers before him had analyzed the concept of substance, Aristotle's theory made a significant contribution to the debate by raising problems and presenting new interpretations of such concepts as form, which philosophers had not addressed before.

---

1. Aristotle, *Metaphysics*, trans. William David Ross, in *The Complete Works of Aristotle: The Revised Oxford Translation*, ed. Jonathan Barnes (Princeton, NJ: Princeton University Press, 1984), 2: 1553–4.
2. Theodore Scaltsas, *Substances and Universals in Aristotle's Metaphysics* (New York: Cornell

University Press, 1994), 72.
3. Aristotle, *Metaphysics*, 2: 1623.
4. Christopher Shields, *Aristotle* (London: Routledge, 2007), 232–4.
5. Alan Code, "Aristotle's Logic and Metaphysics, " in *Routledge History of Philosophy, Volume II: From Aristotle to Augustine*, ed. David Furley (London: Routledge, 1999), 54.
6. Aristotle, *Metaphysics*, 2: 1706.
7. W. K. C. Guthrie, *The Greek Philosophers: From Thales to Aristotle* (London: Routledge, 2013), 121.

SECTION 2
IDEAS

MODULE 5
MAIN IDEAS

KEY POINTS

- Broadly speaking, the main theme of *Metaphysics* is "being"—specifically as it concerns substance.*
- Substance, according to Aristotle, is the form immanent* in matter. That means, it only exists in matter.
- Aristotle's style makes his complex arguments hard to follow. The coherence of *Metaphysics* as a whole has also been compromised by translation issues.

Key Themes

Broadly speaking, the main theme of Aristotle's *Metaphysics* is being. The author explains that metaphysics* is a science of "being qua being"* (being by virtue of being) and makes a contrast between his inquiry into being and specific sciences such as geometry or physics.[1] In this way, he unites the books of *Metaphysics* by this common theme. As Irish philosopher Terence Irwin* explains, "whatever their literary origins, all these books have a common subject matter, since they all contribute to the universal science that studies the common presuppositions of the other sciences."[2] Specific sciences analyze particular aspects of being, while Aristotle's science, typically referred to as "ontology"* today, concentrates on existence itself. Aristotle discusses the general theme of being in *Metaphysics* by engaging with such themes as substance, change, and the notion of the unmoved mover.*

Aristotle claims that the investigation of being amounts to the investigation of substance.[3] Interestingly, only the central books of *Metaphysics*—Zeta, Eta, and Theta—address substance as the main theme. The contents of Beta, Gamma, Epsilon, Lambda, Mu, and Nu supplement this discussion in various ways by addressing more or less loosely related topics. The books Delta, which discusses philosophical vocabulary, and Kappa—which contains summaries of Aristotle's ideas from *Metaphysics* and his other work, *Physics*—do not relate to the main discussion of substance in any obvious way.

> "The formula in which the term itself is not present but its meaning is expressed, this is the formula of the essence of each thing."
>
> —— Aristotle, *Metaphysics.*

Exploring the Ideas

We can best understand substances as "ontologically basic entities":[4] that is, the essences of objects. For Aristotle, substances are also principles and causes of being.[5] In *Metaphysics* book Zeta, Aristotle develops a hylomorphic* theory. This theory states that substance is a form present in matter.[6] The formula of this definition is quite nuanced. Rejecting the idea that substance is simply a compound comprising form and matter, Aristotle notes that a compound cannot exist before its constituent parts.[7] The actual substance is a form, but it must be present in matter, because, according to Aristotle, forms are immanent: that is, they do not have independent existence and can only be found in objects. The form of a man, for example, can only be found in a man.

This does not mean, however, that every man has his own peculiar form. A form, according to Aristotle, is an essence, which he defines as "the formula in which the term itself is not present but its meaning is expressed, this is the formula of the essence of each thing."[8] Marc Cohen,* a contemporary philosopher working on Aristotle, suggests that we may best understand this complex definition by considering an essence as equivalent to an object's species.[9] A form present in a particular man gives him essential properties necessary for being a man, but it does not determine his accidental features, for instance the shape of his nose.

Language and Expression

Aristotle's surviving works remain notoriously difficult to read. In *Metaphysics*, he uses highly technical, jargon-filled language and presents his very complex ideas in terse, dense prose. One reason for this may be that he wrote these works as lecture notes for himself, and perhaps for his pupils—"the Aristotelian Corpus, as we have it, largely consists of works that appear to be closely related to Aristotle's lectures."[10] Any student who has tried to make sense of another student's notes can appreciate the challenge Aristotle has left us.

Metaphysics also lacks continuous and coherent narrative—another reason readers find it difficult to understand. We can read most of its books as self-contained and independent treatises.

Scholars have not clarified how—or if—Aristotle intended the topics in separate books to complement each other. But at the same time, *Metaphysics* as a whole does have some coherence. We may read it as a collection of different approaches exploring various questions relating to the notion of being. As John Ackrill, * a twentieth-century classicist and philosopher, describes it, Aristotle's philosophy "is not a single, rigid system; nor can the treatises be set out and expounded in a simple chronological order. The real unity in his work is to be found in method, style and intellectual character, and in the pervasiveness of some terminology."[11]

The terminology Aristotle uses in *Metaphysics* has played a role in the development of philosophical vocabulary. "Much of the technical vocabulary of later philosophy is derived from Latin versions of Aristotle's metaphysical terms: for example, 'substance', 'essence', 'quality', 'quantity' and 'category.'"[12] Many, if not all, of the terms we use to describe fundamental reality today were first defined and used in *Metaphysics*. For that reason and many others, the work has an important place in the history of philosophy.

---

1. Aristotle, *Metaphysics*, trans. William David Ross, in *The Complete Works of Aristotle: The Revised Oxford Translation*, ed. Jonathan Barnes (Princeton, NJ: Princeton University Press, 1984), 2: 1584.
2. Terence Irwin, "Aristotle, " in *The Shorter Routledge Encyclopedia of Philosophy*, ed. Edward Craig (London: Routledge, 2005), 56.
3. Aristotle, *Metaphysics*, 2: 1624.
4. Michael J. Loux, *Primary "Ousia": An Essay on Aristotle's Metaphysics Z and H* (Ithaca, NY:

Cornell University Press, 1991), 2.
5. Aristotle, *Metaphysics*, 2: 1643.
6. Aristotle, *Metaphysics*, 2: 1644.
7. Aristotle, *Metaphysics*, 2: 1624.
8 Aristotle, *Metaphysics*, 2: 1626.
9. S. Marc Cohen, "Substances, " in *A Companion to Aristotle*, ed. Georgios Anagnostopoulis (Malden, MA: Wiley-Blackwell, 2009), 203.
10. Terence Irwin and Gail Fine, *Aristotle: Introductory Readings* (Indianapolis, IN: Hackett Publishing Company; 1996), 12.
11. J. L. Ackrill, *Aristotle the Philosopher* (Oxford: Oxford University Press, 1981), 4.
12. David Furley, introduction to *Routledge History of Philosophy, Volume II: From Aristotle to Augustine*, ed. David Furley (London: Routledge, 1999), 4.

MODULE 6
SECONDARY IDEAS

KEY POINTS

* Aristotle introduced the notions of "potentiality"* and "actuality"* to help him offer a solution to Parmenides'* paradox of change. He also introduces the concept of a first cause and of an unmoved mover.*
* These concepts explore different aspects of being, apart from the notion of substance, * but they are very important in their own right.
* Aristotle's ideas on these notions are classic studies of some of the foundational questions of metaphysics.*

Other Ideas

The main idea Aristotle tackles in *Metaphysics* is substance. But concepts such as "potentiality" and "actuality, " as well as the nature of God, also contribute to his project of investigating "being qua being."*1 Aristotle develops his ideas of potentiality and actuality most clearly in his other work, *Physics*. He used these concepts to answer the philosophical problem of change, a question the pre-Socratic* philosopher Parmenides* had raised.

In a notoriously complicated argument, Parmenides maintained that one cannot use the notion of non-being to explain being, since non-being does not exist. Ultimately, this led him to assert that change is impossible, because change involves the generation and destruction of states. "Parmenides rejected pluralism and the reality of any kind of change: for him all was one indivisible, unchanging reality, and any appearances to the contrary were illusions, to be dispelled by reason and revelation."[2]

Because they did not accept the existence of non-being, both Parmenides and Plato* (especially in his middle works) were of the opinion that generation—the act of coming into being from a state of non-being—is impossible. Following that logic, since destruction requires the change from being into non-being, destruction is equally impossible.

In *Metaphysics* book Theta, Aristotle offers an account of change that solves Parmenides' puzzle by distinguishing between being-as-potentiality and being-as-actuality.[3] A child, for instance, exists potentially as an adult and in actuality as a child. As Aristotle saw it, change is not a phenomenon in which non-existence comes into existence, but in which "being potentially" changes into "being actually."

> *"One actuality always precedes another in time right back to the actuality of the eternal prime mover."*
>
> —— Aristotle, *Metaphysics*

Exploring the Ideas

In *Metaphysics* book Theta, Aristotle uses the concepts of potentiality and actuality to explain the relationship between matter and form in their compound (or amalgamated) existence. According to him, form is actuality and matter is potentiality.[4] For example, an actual block of wood has a potential existence as a statue, because a sculptor can carve it into one. Aristotle held that actuality always precedes potentiality: "one actuality always precedes another in time right back to the actuality of the eternal prime mover."[5] This leads us to the second important idea Aristotle presents in *Metaphysics*: the prime concept of the unmoved mover.

In *Metaphysics* book Alpha, Aristotle states that gods are the first causes and principles.[6] He elaborates on this idea in book Lambda. First, Aristotle discusses the nature of change as a kind of motion.[7] Then he investigates the types of motion, so he may determine the first cause of all the motion. Aristotle concludes that, "there is, then, something which is always moved with an unceasing motion, which is motion in a circle; and this is plain not in theory only but in fact. Therefore the first heavens must be eternal. There is therefore also something which moves them. And since that which is moved and moves is intermediate, there is a mover which moves without being moved, being eternal, substance, and actuality."[8] This motion is not physical. The unmoved mover causes motion just as desired objects move those who desire them.[9] Aristotle then considers whether there are many unmoved movers or only one.[10] His conclusion about this remains unclear. As philosophy professor Terence Irwin* points out, in *Metaphysics* Lambda Aristotle argues that the movements of every astronomical body originate from a separate unmoved mover, but later he also states that, "the universe is unified by a single first unmoved mover." These two claims remain difficult to reconcile.[11]

Aristotle's original and innovative ideas about change and the unmoved mover solved known philosophical problems in his time. They also stand as substantial contributions to philosophical debates right to the present day.

Overlooked

Aristotle's *Metaphysics* covers many themes and contains multiple arguments. In part, this accounts for its popularity through the ages. Anyone interested in metaphysics and its history will seek out and analyze *Metaphysics*. In thousands of years of analysis, scholars have not overlooked much about this work. Its central topics—substance, change, essence, God—and Aristotle's smaller observations and inferences, such as the ideas that the object can be more than the sum of its parts, [12] have been studied meticulously.

At the same time, there is still room to discover and reinterpret certain topics Aristotle covers in *Metaphysics*. American philosopher Jonathan Beere's* book *Doing and Being: An Interpretation of Aristotle's Metaphysics Theta*[13] examines Aristotle's use of the terms *energeia* and *dunamis* in *Metaphysics*. A simple explanation is that *energeia* is actuality and *dunamis* means potentiality but Aristotle used these terms in very complicated ways and it is difficult to give their precise theoretical definitions. By means of careful analysis of the ways in which Aristotle uses these terms and the ways in which he describes them theoretically, Beere resolves major arguments from *Metaphysics* Theta.

---

1. Aristotle, *Metaphysics*, trans. William David Ross, in *The Complete Works of Aristotle: The*

Revised Oxford Translation, ed. Jonathan Barnes (Princeton, NJ: Princeton University Press, 1984), 2: 1584.
2. Nick Huggett, "Zeno's Paradoxes, " *Stanford Encyclopedia of Philosophy*, accessed February 11, 2015, http: //plato.stanford.edu/entries/paradox- zeno/.
3. Aristotle, *Metaphysics*, 2: 1656–7.
4. Aristotle, *Metaphysics*, 2: 1659.
5. Aristotle, *Metaphysics*, 2: 1659.
6. Aristotle, *Metaphysics*, 2: 1555.
7. Aristotle, *Metaphysics*, 2: 1690.
8. Aristotle, Metaphysics, 2: 1694.
9. Aristotle, *Metaphysics*, 2: 1694.
10. Aristotle, Metaphysics, 2: 1697–8.
11. Terence Irwin, "Aristotle, " in *The Shorter Routledge Encyclopedia of Philosophy*, ed. Edward Craig (London: Routledge, 2005), 59.
12. Aristotle, *Metaphysics*, 2: 1650.
13. Jonathan Beere, *Doing and Being: An Interpretation of Aristotle's Metaphysics Theta* (Oxford: Oxford University Press, 2009).

MODULE 7
ACHIEVEMENT

KEY POINTS

- Aristotle's main achievement in *Metaphysics* is to present a number of thorough, rigorous studies on the theme of being.
- Aristotle's approach and method contributed to the quality and lasting reputation of the work.
- His theory about substance* prevailed for nearly two thousand years, up until the early modern period* (1450–1750).

Assessing the Argument

In composing *Metaphysics,* Aristotle mainly aimed to explore the most fundamental ontological* questions, that is the "causes and principles" of being.¹ But he died before completing *Metaphysics* and left the work somewhat disjointed and lacking in a clear structure. The books Beta, Gamma, Epsilon, Zeta, Eta, and Theta clearly explore ontological topics, especially the issue of existence. The rest of the books treat topics that are not obvious parts of the main discussion.

Aristotle did not decide on the order of the books as we read them today. About three centuries after his death, the Roman editor Andronicus* collected Aristotle's treatises on related topics and published them under the title of *Metaphysics*. For this reason, we cannot know what Aristotle intended his finished account to achieve. Most likely, he wanted to produce a study of the fundamental nature of everything that exists, and in doing so, to introduce and develop a thorough understanding of philosophy's most fundamental questions, such as what a substance is, how to explain change, and how to understand first causes.

The ideas in *Metaphysics* do have a certain conceptual unity. All the books contain discussions relating to metaphysics.* While Aristotle does not always link the arguments to one another explicitly, *Metaphysics* remains a compelling collection of studies on the nature of being.

To the extent that Aristotle set out to provide an account of being, his work remains very successful. He not only engaged with some of the most difficult metaphysical questions, he also proposed possible answers. His strong, compelling ontological account rivals the Platonic* metaphysics of his day and has been recognized as an important contribution to metaphysics for centuries. Aristotle translator Joe Sachs notes, "when Aristotle articulated the central question of the group of writings we know as his *Metaphysics*, he said it was a question that would never cease to raise itself. He was right. He also regarded his own contributions to the handling of that question as belonging to the final phase of responding to it. I think he was right about that too. The *Metaphysics* is one of the most helpful books there is for contending with a question the asking of which is one of the things that makes us human."[2]

> "When Aristotle articulated the central question of the group of writings we know as his Metaphysics, he said it was a question that would never cease to raise itself. He was right. He also regarded his own contributions to the handling of that question as belonging to the final phase of responding to it. I think he was right about that too. The Metaphysics is

one of the most helpful books there is for contending with a question the asking of which is one of the things that makes us human."

— Joe Sachs, "Aristotle: Metaphysics"

Achievement in Context

In his lifetime and in ours, *Metaphysics* has remained popular, as have Aristotle's other works. Some scholars used to argue that after the death of his close followers, Aristotle's works became virtually forgotten until they were published in the Roman* period. Today scholars generally agree that Aristotle's ideas were known throughout the Hellenistic period*—the three centuries between the death of Alexander the Great* and the rise of the ancient Roman Empire.[3]

Metaphysics also exerted a great influence on early Islamic* philosophers. Important thinkers, such as the early twelfth-century legal scholar and philosopher Averroes (Ibn Rushd), * wrote commentaries on Aristotle's work and used his concepts in their own works. While Aristotle and other ancient philosophers were hardly known in the early Middle Ages* (beginning in the twelfth century C.E.), Aristotle's works gradually became more widely available in Europe. This re-emergence of Aristotle's writings set off great interest in his thought among European thinkers.

The main topic of Aristotle's *Metaphysics*—substance—has remained a classic metaphysical notion and a central concern of metaphysics since the time he first discussed it. Philosophers in the ancient world, and those in the Middle Ages, considered *Metaphysics* a work of great importance. Aristotle's account of substance as a form present in matter rivaled the earlier Platonic idea that substances must be incorporeal, * timeless forms existing outside the tangible world. Ancient and medieval* metaphysicians debated the merits of Plato's* or Aristotle's accounts of substance and used them as reference points to construct their own accounts. This is why the text maintained a central role in philosophical debates for many centuries.

Limitations

One might describe *Metaphysics* as the product of its time, because it concerns itself with topics that were most relevant to philosophers in the Classical period.* But nonetheless, it remained an important work for many centuries after Aristotle wrote it.

In the modern period, however, a critique issued by the eighteenth-century Scottish philosopher David Hume* challenged the work's relevance. Hume argued that because Aristotle had not based his notion of substance on any evidence, philosophers should discard it. Instead, Hume proposed a so-called bundle theory: * essences of objects are nothing but the sum of all their properties.[4] Aristotle believed that particular properties of a man, such as a snub nose or height, do not explain what it is to be a man. However, Hume argued the opposite. This criticism did not erase Aristotle from philosophical debate completely, but it did substantially diminish his influence. More importantly, the focus of philosophical discussions began to shift. With Hume's rejection of the very notion of substance, philosophers started investigating alternative ways of accounting for what the essence of being is. Eventually, scholars began to class Aristotle's thought under "history of philosophy." *Metaphysics* and his other works no longer appeared to be at the cutting edge of the discipline.

---

1. Aristotle, *Metaphysics*, trans. William David Ross, in *The Complete Works of Aristotle: The Revised Oxford Translation*, ed. Jonathan Barnes (Princeton, NJ: Princeton University Press, 1984), 2: 1553.
2. Joe Sachs, "Aristotle: Metaphysics, " Internet Encyclopedia of Philosophy, accessed February 10, 2015, http: //www.iep.utm.edu/aris-met/.
3. Jonathan Barnes, "Life and work, " in *The Cambridge Companion to Aristotle*, ed. Jonathan Barnes (Cambridge: Cambridge University Press, 1995), 10–11.
4. See, for instance, David Hume, *Treatise* 1.4.6.3.

MODULE 8
PLACE IN THE AUTHOR'S WORK

KEY POINTS
- Aristotle wrote a huge number of treatises on a wide variety of topics.
- He also looks into the central topics of *Metaphysics* in his books *Categories* and *Physics*.
- *Metaphysics* remains one of Aristotle's best-known and most important works.

Positioning

When did Aristotle compose *Metaphysics*? Scholars have debated this question extensively. Until the twentieth century, academics viewed Aristotle's works as a consistent and finished whole—treating the entire Aristotelian corpus as the product of a mature thinker. Over the last 100 years, however, scholars have challenged this view and it is now generally rejected. Thomas Case,* an early twentieth-century philosopher who worked on Aristotle, argued that it would have taken Aristotle many years to produce the sheer volume of works he authored. So it remains unlikely he composed them all at the end of his life. Instead, Case argues that Aristotle kept his works as manuscripts and worked on them continuously throughout his career.[1]

The lack of unity among the books of *Metaphysics* also supports this interpretation. The variety of topics and their lack of coherent connections clearly indicates that Aristotle did not produce *Metaphysics* in a conventional manner—writing the entire work at once. So it may well have been composed over a longer time period. Jonathan Barnes, * a well-known Aristotelian scholar, has pointed out that ancient commentaries on *Metaphysics* imply that Aristotle died before editing the work properly, leaving it in an incoherent state.² Overall, scholars tend to agree that *Metaphysics* must have been a product of continuous work throughout Aristotle's lifetime, and that he may indeed have left it unfinished when he died.

The central theme developed in *Metaphysics*, the idea of substance, * can also be found in another of Aristotle's works, *Categories*. Although there is no clear evidence suggesting that Aristotle wrote *Categories* before *Metaphysics*, "it is easier to understand the relation of the doctrine of substance in the *Categories* ... to the doctrine and argument of *Metaphysics* 7 if we supposed that *Metaphysics* 7 is later."³ Students often read *Categories* before *Metaphysics* as an introduction to the notion of substance, because it presents some simpler ideas. For instance, in *Categories*, Aristotle defines substance as that which is capable of receiving contraries while being numerically singular.⁴ To help readers understand this idea, Aristotle provided an example: because a color cannot be black and white while remaining the same color, color is not substance. But a man can be pale and become tanned while remaining the same man. So being a man is a substance. This idea shows that we ought to understand substances as explanations of what it is like to be, for instance, a man. In *Categories,* Aristotle points out that if we wish to know what the essence of being a man is, we cannot simply look at any properties that a man might have. A man can be pale or old or an Athenian citizen, but being pale, old, and an Athenian citizen do not explain what it is to be a man. For this reason, Aristotle suggests that we need to determine what the substance of man is by investigating what aspects of a man persist through all changes.

> "A prodigious researcher and writer, Aristotle left a great body of work, perhaps numbering as many as two-hundred treatises, from which approximately thirty-one survive."
> —— Christopher Shields, "Aristotle" in *Stanford Encyclopedia of Philosophy*

Integration

"A prodigious researcher and writer, Aristotle left a great body of work, perhaps numbering as many as two-hundred treatises, from which approximately thirty-one survive."[5] Although we have only a relatively small portion of Aristotle's works, those surviving texts cover a wide range of topics, from metaphysics* to politics. Even among ancient philosophers who often produced large numbers of wide-ranging treatises, Aristotle's achievement is outstanding.

The range of Aristotle's works can also be useful in helping understand some of his more complex ideas. Scholars and philosophers commonly read and cross-reference works such as *Physics*, *Categories*, (and sometimes even *On the Soul*), and *Metaphysics*. "Some of the basic concepts of the *Categories* and *Physics*—including substance, particular, universal, * form, matter, cause and potentiality—are discussed more fully in the

Metaphysics."⁶ When looking to understand the ideas Aristotle presents in *Metaphysics*, we do well to consider the arguments and ideas in his other works that address the same or similar issues. But it is also possible to read different works together to find out what Aristotle's overall stance was on some general question. For instance, if we want to consider what Aristotle thought about the nature of human beings, we would find it useful to read not only *Metaphysics* or *On the Soul*, but also *Nicomachean Ethics* and *Politics*.

Significance

While Aristotle wrote many groundbreaking treatises in various areas of philosophy, *Metaphysics* is still one of his most important works. Aristotle's innovative way of thinking has made his body of work vastly influential to later philosophers. But even if he had written nothing but *Metaphysics*, Aristotle would have had a great impact in the history of philosophy. First adopted and disseminated by Aristotle's followers, the Peripatetics, * the ideas in *Metaphysics* have resounded through the centuries. Many different people have studied them, from ancient Greek and Roman* philosophers to medieval* thinkers, Islamic* intellectuals, and modern philosophers.

However, because of developments in the discipline of philosophy, Aristotle's influence began to wane during the early modern* period in the mid-fifteenth century. Philosophers largely rejected the topic of substance. This was not only because new theories and ideas had emerged, but also because the philosophical focus started shifting to different topics. This, in turn, decreased Aristotle's relevance. Yet this does not diminish his overall achievement. Even if philosophers no longer accept some of Aristotle's concepts and arguments, he remains one of the most important thinkers in the history of philosophy. Scholars still discuss the historical *and* philosophical importance of certain aspects of his thought. *Categories*, *Physics*, and especially *Metaphysics* earned Aristotle acclaim as one of the most important metaphysicians in Western philosophy.

---

1. Thomas Case, "Aristotle, " in *Aristotle's Philosophical Development: Problems and Prospects*, ed. William Wians (Lanham, MD: Rowman & Littlefield, 1996), 13.
2. Jonathan Barnes, "Roman Aristotle, " in *Philosophia Togata II, Plato and Aristotle at Rome*, ed. Jonathan Barnes and Miriam Griffin (Oxford: Clarendon Press, 1997), 61–2.
3. Terence Irwin, "Aristotle, " in *The Shorter Routledge Encyclopedia of Philosophy*, ed. Edward Craig (London: Routledge, 2005), 51.
4. Aristotle, *Categories*, trans. John L. Ackrill, in *The Complete Works of Aristotle: The Revised Oxford Translation*, ed. Jonathan Barnes (Princeton, NJ: Princeton University Press, 1984), 1: 7.
5. Christopher Shields, "Aristotle, " *Stanford Encyclopedia of Philosophy*, accessed February 10, 2015, http: //plato.stanford.edu/entries/aristotle/.
6. Irwin, "Aristotle, " 56.

SECTION 3
IMPACT

MODULE 9
THE FIRST RESPONSES

KEY POINTS
- Plotinus* criticized Aristotle's views by arguing that failing to include accidental properties* in the notion of substance* leaves one unable to distinguish between individual substances.
- Commentators such as Alexander of Aphrodisias* advocated Aristotle's views against the views of such rival schools as Stoicism.*
- Overall, Aristotle's ideas were very well received and inspired many philosophers to develop their own ideas.

Criticism

In *Metaphysics,* Aristotle criticizes the existing philosophical tradition. But, surprisingly, the author received little explicit criticism himself. In Aristotle's most immediate circle, his own followers—known as the Peripatetics*—appear to have been more interested in preserving his works than debating them. Interestingly, this trend continued even after Aristotle's original Lyceum* school disbanded. In later antiquity, * Aristotle's works became a popular source for commentators such as Alexander of Aphrodisias, who explained Aristotle's views and criticized rival philosophical accounts.

Even the Neoplatonists, * who identified themselves with Plato's* thought, did not reject Aristotle's metaphysics* entirely. Often they studied it alongside Plato's work. Ilsetraut Hadot, * a present-day scholar working on ancient philosophy, has argued that the Neoplatonic philosophers found that Plato's and Aristotle's works could be studied side by side. Yet, "Plato's philosophy, by contrast with Aristotle's, is considered the more elevated, the more theological, the more inspired. It is likewise clear that the *Metaphysics* can only be a half-stage between the studies of natural principles and natural causes, and the true theology developed by Plato in his *Parmenides*. Aristotle's thought is not, by nature, sufficiently 'transcendent'."[1]

One exception to this trend stands out: Plotinus's critique of Aristotle's idea of substance in his seminal work *Enneads*. Plotinus employs various arguments to reject Aristotle's idea that substance is immanent* form, present in matter. He also defends a Platonic* notion of form as existing beyond the sensible world, the world we can see and feel. Lloyd Gerson, * a noted expert on ancient philosophy, has suggested that Plotinus identified a problem with Aristotle's account of substance when he argued that Aristotle could not reasonably maintain that substances are immanent in an object. If we assume that accidental properties* (such as having a snub nose, for example) are not part of the essence, then nothing in the essence requires it to belong to a particular object. For instance, such a notion of essence does not distinguish between Plato and Socrates.* In Plotinus's view, this renders Aristotle's account of substance unjustifiable.[2]

> "Plato's philosophy, by contrast with Aristotle's, is considered the more elevated, the more theological, the more inspired. It is likewise clear that the Metaphysics *can only be a half-stage between the studies of natural principles and natural causes, and the true theology developed by Plato in his* Parmenides. *Aristotle's thought is not, by nature, sufficiently 'transcendent'."*
> ——Ilsetraut Hadot, "The Role of the Commentaries on Aristotle in the Teaching of Philosophy according to the Prefaces of the Neoplatonic Commentaries on the Categories"

Responses

Aristotle did not have a chance to respond to contemporary critiques of *Metaphysics*, because the evidence that exists suggests that most appeared after his death. During his lifetime, Aristotle most probably engaged in many critical debates. He may even have altered his views in response to criticisms, but no evidence of this survives. This lack of evidence makes it impossible to know with absolute certainty how Aristotle might have been criticized and what effect such criticism may have had on him.

After Aristotle's death, his followers, commonly called the Peripatetics, took up the task of promoting Aristotle's thought and responding to criticism. Peripatetic commentators such as Alexander of Aphrodisias, who wrote a commentary on *Metaphysics*, advocated Aristotle's ideas against those of other philosophical schools such as the Stoics. Aristotle's supporters also responded to those who explored the differences between Platonic and Aristotelian thought.

However, these commentators were not necessarily responding to criticism of Aristotle. They were merely addressing alternative theories as other groups raised them. What remains of Stoic thinking, for instance, does not criticize or even mention Aristotle explicitly. But commentaries defending Aristotle against either implicit or perceived criticism allowed his thought to remain relevant long after it was published.

Conflict and Consensus

The ideas Aristotle presented in *Metaphysics* have been widely read, discussed, and debated since antiquity. Philosophers considered Platonism* the main rival for the philosophy Aristotle set out in the work. That said, even thinkers with Platonic or other philosophical leanings appreciated *Metaphysics*. The critical debate with the Platonists did not necessarily affect the work's reception, either in Aristotle's time or afterwards. We can best understand the rivalry between Platonism and Aristotelianism as an ongoing discussion of the advantages and shortcomings of both these schools of thought. Nobody on either side of the debate denied either theory completely.

Many important thinkers have mounted interesting defenses of Aristotle-inspired metaphysics. According to the Canadian philosopher Claude Panaccio, * the thirteenth-century cleric Thomas Aquinas* "rejected Platonism for having wrongly supposed that universals* have to exist in a separate manner in the extra-mental world to be correctly isolated by the mind ... Even though universals in the strict sense exist only in the mind for him, they nevertheless have an external foundation within the singular things: human nature is somehow in each singular human being."[3]

As Panaccio's modern analysis makes clear, Aristotelian views were talked about and discussed for many centuries after Aristotle's death. And a lively debate still rages between thinkers who sympathize with Aristotle's ideas and those who favor Platonic or Neoplatonic theories. Although some thinkers claimed to have definitively refuted Aristotle's metaphysical account, later philosophers revived and defended it, allowing it to inspire new thought.

---

1. Ilsetraut Hadot, "The Role of the Commentaries on Aristotle in the Teaching of Philosophy according to the Prefaces of the Neoplatonic Commentaries on the Categories, " *Oxford Studies of Ancient Philosophy* supp. vol. (1991): 184.
2. Lloyd Gerson, *Plotinus* (London and New York: Routledge, 1994), 93–6.
3. Claude Panaccio, "Medieval Metaphysics 1: The Problem of Universals, " in *The Routledge Companion to Metaphysics*, ed. Robin Le Poidevin et al. (London and New York: Routledge, 2009), 52.

MODULE 10
THE EVOLVING DEBATE

KEY POINTS
- Aristotle's *Metaphysics* played an important role in the works of later thinkers such as Thomas Aquinas* and Avicenna (Ibn Sīnā).*
- Aristotle's followers, the Peripatetics, * formed a school of thought, but it did not last beyond the Hellenistic period.*
- *Metaphysics* played an important role in the development of the discipline that took its name from the book. Aristotle's work introduced new ideas and arguments that became central to the field and inspired various philosophers to go on to produce their own analyses of its topics.

Uses and Problems

Aristotle's *Metaphysics* greatly influenced the evolution of philosophy in general, and in particular of the discipline that came to be called "metaphysics."* Aristotle's critique of Plato's* idea that substances* are incorporeal* forms played an especially important role in the development of metaphysics.

For later philosophers, such as Neoplatonists* or medieval* metaphysicians, the Platonic* and Aristotelian accounts of substance represented a great dilemma. While Plato theorized that incorporeal, eternal forms exist as substances, Aristotle's account suggests that substances only exist as immanent* forms—that is, as forms existing in matter. Philosophers saw both accounts as important, yet they remained incompatible. This incompatibility led to a great debate among thinkers. Some chose one of the views and defended it against the other. Others chose to sidestep the problem and develop an account that approached the idea of being in an entirely different manner. As British philosopher David Sedley* notes: "Platonism* and Aristotelianism were to become the dominant philosophies of the Western tradition from the second century A.D. at least until the end of the Renaissance, * and the legacy of both remains central to Western philosophy today."[1]

Aristotle's thought was also very important for the Islamic* philosophical tradition. His metaphysics influenced such prominent thinkers as the tenth-century C.E. Persian physician Ibn Sīnā (or, in Latinate form, Avicenna). Together with other Islamic philosophers, Ibn Sīnā read *Metaphysics* as an important foundational work in ontology, * and also used Aristotelian concepts, such as substance, to develop his own original ideas. Ibn Sīnā wrote three encyclopedias. The first of these, *al-Shifa'* (*The Cure*), is "a work modelled on the corpus of the philosopher, namely, Aristotle, that covers the natural sciences, logic, mathematics, metaphysics and theology."[2]

Philosophers in medieval Europe also considered *Metaphysics* a foundational text and debated the differences between Platonism and Aristotelianism and their respective views on the nature of substance. Medieval metaphysicians often adopted one of the two accounts and presented their own notions based on it. Possibly the most famous medieval philosopher influenced by Aristotle was the thirteenth-century Italian cleric Thomas Aquinas: "every part of Aquinas' philosophy is imbued with metaphysical principles, many of which are recognizably Aristotelian. Consequently, concepts such as potentiality and actuality, * matter and form, substance, essence ...—all of which are fundamental in Aquinas' metaphysics—should be considered in their original Aristotelian context."³

Aristotle's works—including *Metaphysics*—continue to influence philosophers today, especially those who defend a view that substances or essential properties exist that are distinct from merely accidental properties.*

> "Platonism and Aristotelianism were to become the dominant philosophies of the Western tradition from the second century A.D. at least until the end of the Renaissance, and the legacy of both remains central to Western philosophy today."
> ——David Sedley, from "Ancient Philosophy" in *Routledge Encyclopedia of Philosophy*

Schools of Thought

Aristotle's own philosophical school, the Lyceum, * lasted only a short time. His works, including *Metaphysics*, were at first read only in the school he founded. But around three centuries later, a Roman editor, Andronicus, * collected and published them. In the intervening period Aristotle received less attention than during his lifetime, but Andronicus's publication revived interest in his thought.

After Aristotle died in 322 B.C.E., his followers—the Peripatetics—kept the Lyceum going. But they saw their most important work as preserving Aristotle's legacy and working in the tradition of his thought.

As the well-known Aristotelian scholar Robert Sharples* notes, the early Peripatetics were most interested in gathering information in various fields of study and resolving theoretical difficulties. The school became less popular during the Hellenistic period, but continued until the Romans conquered Athens* in the first century B.C.E.

The second wave of interest in Aristotelian thought happened about 300 years later, during the Roman period, * possibly when Andronicus published Aristotle's works. The increasing number of commentaries on his works at this time demonstrates Aristotle's hold on a new generation of philosophers. Among those whose work survives, the best-known commentator is Alexander of Aphrodisias, * who wrote about *Metaphysics* in particular.

After antiquity, * the period of Western civilization before the Middle Ages, * philosophers discussed Aristotle's ideas less frequently in the philosophical context in which he had presented them. Instead, thinkers applied the concepts that he introduced to a variety of philosophical issues. We cannot call these later thinkers Aristotle's "followers, " but his work clearly influenced them as they developed their own views. For instance, medieval logicians (people studying or skilled in logic) applied Aristotle's concepts of matter and form to explain syllogisms, the logical process where two general statements lead to a more particular statement.[4]

Irish philosopher Terence Irwin* suggests, "modern historical study of Aristotle begins in the nineteenth century. It has led to philosophical reassessment, and his works have once again become a source of philosophical insight and argument. Many of the themes of Aristotelian philosophy—the nature of substance, the relation of form to matter ... —have reappeared as issues in philosophical debates, and Aristotle's contribution to these debates has influenced the course of philosophical discussion."[5]

In Current Scholarship

Overall, Aristotle's *Metaphysics* enjoys great popularity among philosophers, historians of philosophy, and intellectuals today. Contemporary thinkers often use the ideas presented in *Metaphysics* to inspire their own theories. But scholars still approach *Metaphysics* exegetically* as well—using critical analysis and careful study to work out its original meaning. Whatever their purpose in reading *Metaphysics*, the work remains extremely important, not only for the development of the discipline it gave its name to, but also as a philosophical work in its own right.

In the various guides to *Metaphysics*, such as British scholar Jonathan Barnes's* *Cambridge Companion to Aristotle*[6] and John Ackrill's* *Aristotle the Philosopher*[7] or Michael Loux's *Primary "Ousia": An Essay on Aristotle's Metaphysics Z and H*,[8] scholars look for the most accurate interpretation of the ideas found in *Metaphysics*, attempting to uncover Aristotle's original meaning. This approach involves not only interpreting ideas, but also investigating the circumstances surrounding how the text was written. For instance, scholars generally agree that Aristotle wrote the books of *Metaphysics* himself; but did Aristotle put them into their existing order or was that done by later editors? This question is still open to debate. But historically minded interpreters such as Barnes concern themselves primarily with the question of how *Metaphysics* itself ought to be understood.

---

1. David Sedley, "Ancient Philosophy, " in *The Shorter Routledge Encyclopedia of Philosophy*, ed. Edward Craig (London: Routledge, 2005), 17.
2. Sajjad Rizvi, "Avicenna (Ibn Sīnā), " Internet Encyclopedia of Philosophy, accessed February 11, 2015, http: //www.iep.utm.edu/avicenna/.
3. Norman Kretzmann and Eleonore Stump, "Thomas Aquinas, " in *The Shorter Routledge Encyclopedia of Philosophy*, ed. Edward Craig (London: Routledge, 2005), 36.
4. Paul Thom, "Logical Form, " in *The Handbook of Medieval Philosophy*, ed. John Marenbon (Oxford: Oxford University Press, 2013), 273.
5. Terence Irwin, "Aristotle, " in *The Shorter Routledge Encyclopedia of Philosophy*, ed. Edward Craig (London: Routledge, 2005), 67.
6. Jonathan Barnes, ed., *The Cambridge Companion to Aristotle* (Cambridge: Cambridge University Press, 1995).
7. J. L. Ackrill, *Aristotle the Philosopher* (Oxford: Oxford University Press, 1981).
8. Michael Loux, *Primary "Ousia": An Essay on Aristotle's Metaphysics Z and H* (Ithaca, NY: Cornell University Press, 1991).

MODULE 11
IMPACT AND INFLUENCE TODAY

KEY POINTS

* Today *Metaphysics* is considered a classic in the field of metaphysics.*
* The philosophical position called essentialism* derives from Aristotle's work, and it has been both criticized and defended over the last few hundred years.
* A revival of interest in metaphysics during the latter half of the twentieth century has led to more contemporary philosophers looking to Aristotle for ideas and inspiration.

Position

Widely recognized as one of the most important works in the history of philosophy—especially the discipline that took its name from the book—Aristotle's *Metaphysics* remains important today, almost two thousand years after he wrote it.

Contemporary philosophers still find some of Aristotle's arguments substantial enough to use as inspiration. In some cases, Aristotle's ideas even serve as a platform for developing new ideas. The combination of these two factors makes Aristotle "... among the greatest philosophers of all time. Judged solely in terms of his philosophical influence, only Plato is his peer: Aristotle's works shaped centuries of philosophy from Late Antiquity through the Renaissance, * and even today continue to be studied with keen, non-antiquarian interest."[1]

As for Aristotle's influence in contemporary debates, philosophers fall into two camps. On the one hand, philosophers no longer consider some of the central topics that Aristotle looks at in *Metaphysics*, such as substance, * to be significant. But there was a revival of interest in metaphysics in the second half of the twentieth century. As a result, contemporary metaphysicians turn to Aristotle's ideas as inspiration and as a point of reference. John Ackrill, * a classicist and philosopher, notes that the "topics of very many books and articles published since then are straight out of Aristotle. Things and qualities, matter and change, count-nouns and mass-words, subject and predicate: such topics are at the centre of Aristotle's investigation and his approach to them has the same linguistic emphasis and sensitivity as that of recent metaphysicians."[2]

> "Aristotle numbers among the greatest philosophers of all time. Judged solely in terms of his philosophical influence, only Plato is his peer: Aristotle's works shaped centuries of philosophy from Late Antiquity through the Renaissance, and even today continue to be studied with keen, non-antiquarian interest ... His extant writings span a wide range of disciplines, from logic, metaphysics and philosophy of mind, through ethics ... In all these areas, Aristotle's theories have provided illumination, met with resistance, sparked debate, and generally stimulated the sustained interest of an abiding readership."
>
> —— Christopher Shields, "Aristotle" in *Stanford Encyclopedia of Philosophy*.

Interaction

Ideas found in Aristotle's *Metaphysics* still challenge and influence contemporary philosophical debates. But today's philosophers rarely use Aristotle's arguments directly. The way he discussed philosophical issues differs starkly from the way modern philosophers ask questions. Some of the concepts, theoretical assumptions, and even philosophical methods popular today cannot be found in Aristotle. Yet philosophers still draw useful and inspiring content from works like *Metaphysics* by approaching Aristotle in a loose and interpretative way. For instance, Aristotle's notion of the difference between substantial and accidental properties* inspired the modern theory of essentialism, which holds that every entity has certain core attributes that constitute its identity and function.

Essentialism challenges such popular ideas as bundle theory.* This theory, introduced by Scottish Enlightenment* philosopher David Hume* in the eighteenth century, states that objects are just sums of their properties and no additional entities—such as substances or essential properties—are involved in forming an identity of an object.[3] The recent revival of interest in essentialism and Aristotle's ideas about substances shows that although bundle theory has been popular for several centuries, philosophers can challenge it by reinterpreting ancient ideas (like those of Aristotle) to fit the context of contemporary metaphysics.

The Continuing Debate

In 1973 the American bioethicist Baruch Brody* published an article entitled "Why Settle for Anything Less than Good Old-Fashioned Aristotelian essentialism?" Brody defended a view that there is a distinction between accidental and essential properties that resembles Aristotle's idea of substance. According to Brody, Aristotle correctly noted that some properties are essential in a sense that they constitute what it means to be, for instance, a man. Brody uses the tools of contemporary analytic philosophy* to show the advantages of the notion of essential properties, loosely derived from Aristotle's *Metaphysics*. Similarly, American philosophers Joshua Hoffman* and Gary Rosenkrantz* have also defended the notion of substance. They start by analyzing Aristotle's concept of substance and ultimately reject it for being insufficiently detailed for contemporary metaphysics; but Aristotle's ideas clearly inspired their own account.[4]

The advocates of essentialism remain a minority, yet philosophers recognize they have made important contributions to metaphysical debates about the nature and identity of properties. By interpreting *Metaphysics* broadly, modern philosophers have been able to use its ideas in contemporary thought. In this way *Metaphysics* remains significant not only as a work that helped to shape the field of metaphysics, but also as a source of ideas considered interesting and persuasive even today.

---

1. Christopher Shields, "Aristotle, " *Stanford Encyclopedia of Philosophy*, accessed February 10, 2015, http: //plato.stanford.edu/entries/aristotle/.
2. J. L. Ackrill, *Aristotle the Philosopher* (Oxford: Oxford University Press, 1981), 8.
3. See, for instance, David Hume, *Treatise* 1.4.6.3.
4. Joshua Hoffman and Gary S. Rosenkrantz, *Substance: Its Nature and Existence* (London and New York: Routledge, 1997).

MODULE 12
WHERE NEXT?

KEY POINTS
* *Metaphysics* is very likely to remain a key work in the field.
* It will be studied both for its historic and its philosophical value.
* Few other works have had such a profound influence on the development of the field of metaphysics* specifically, and philosophical debate more generally.

Potential

Aristotle's *Metaphysics* has played a significant role in philosophical discussions ever since it was produced. It is likely to remain a very important work for philosophers and other thinkers.

Metaphysics was an essential influence in the development of this branch of philosophy in the ancient world, as well as in medieval* Western and Islamic* philosophy. Most, if not all, philosophers from these traditions learned from and were inspired by Aristotle's work. As British philosopher Jonathan Barnes* put it, "an account of Aristotle's intellectual afterlife would be little less than a history of European thought."[1]

Today we seem to be in the midst of a more general revival of interest in Aristotelian philosophy. American philosopher Edward Feser* comments that, "while it would certainly be an overstatement to say that a full-scale revival of Aristotelianism is currently underway, it does seem that some of the various strands of thought alluded to are at least beginning to coalesce into something like a self-conscious movement."[2]

Metaphysics has remained at the center of scholarly attention because of its philosophical content. Today, the text has a somewhat more limited influence than in previous generations. Contemporary philosophers generally consider Aristotle's main topic—substance*—a somewhat outdated concept.

Because contemporary concerns diverge from ancient ones, thinkers inspired by Aristotle's metaphysical doctrines today do not typically use his exact arguments. Instead, they use concepts that Aristotle introduced, such as the notion of essence, being, hylomorphism, * or potentiality and actuality.* Reinterpreting these concepts, modern philosophers incorporate them into discussions of contemporary issues. Since Aristotle's *Metaphysics* is a large and complex work, future philosophers are likely to continue to find inspiration in its pages.

> "An account of Aristotle's intellectual afterlife would be little less than a history of European thought."
> ——Jonathan Barnes, *A Very Short Introduction to Aristotle*

Future Directions

Aristotle's *Metaphysics* continues to be essential reading for philosophers, historians of philosophy, and intellectuals. Believing the work occupies an important place not only in the development of metaphysics, but as a philosophical work in its own right, thinkers interested in *Metaphysics* for exegetical* reasons attempt to interpret the text in a way that allows them to uncover Aristotle's original meaning. This approach involves not only interpreting his ideas, but also investigating the circumstances surrounding the text's composition. Scholars generally agree that Aristotle himself wrote the books of *Metaphysics* but they disagree on whether Aristotle or later editors put them into their existing order.

In contrast, historically minded interpreters generally focus on the question of how we should understand *Metaphysics*. The best examples of this approach can be found in various studies and commentaries such as scholar Jonathan Beere's* *Doing and Being: An Interpretation of Aristotle's Metaphysics Theta*[3] or philosopher David Bostock's* translation and commentary on *Metaphysics* books Zeta and Eta.[4]

Other contemporary thinkers use the ideas presented in *Metaphysics* as inspiration for their own theories. Typically less concerned with Aristotle's original meaning, these scholars evaluate and debate the philosophy of Aristotle's ideas. Recently, for example, the American philosophers Joshua Hoffman* and Gary Rosenkrantz* argued that the notion of a substance—and especially the Aristotelian distinction between substance and accidental properties*—is not only philosophically interesting, but in their view it is, in fact, preferable to metaphysical accounts that reject the existence of substances.[5] After discussing Aristotle's ideas, Hoffman and Rosenkrantz introduced their own ideas that were influenced by Aristotle's account of substance.

Contemporary Finnish philosopher Tuomas Tahko* also has a continuing interest in Aristotle's *Metaphysics*. In his most recent work, he argued that accepting the Aristotelian notion of metaphysics as "the first philosophy" is useful when thinking about the scope of contemporary metaphysics.[6]

These modern works show that two millennia after its composition, *Metaphysics* continues to be of great importance for philosophy.

Summary

Aristotle's *Metaphysics* has been central to the development of philosophical ideas for close to two thousand years. Scholars today read and discuss this seminal work not only because it plays a very important role in the history of philosophy, but also because the ideas it presents continue to crop up in philosophical debates. Even contemporary thinkers find inspiration in Aristotle's ancient concepts and arguments.

Aristotle's *Metaphysics* is a unique work that combines shrewd philosophical ideas and rigorous arguments. It has influenced the development of metaphysics more than any other existing work of antiquity.* As it appeals to a range of thinkers from different cultural backgrounds and historical periods, Aristotle's text is likely to remain important. His notions such as "being qua being, "* substance, hylomorphism, and potentiality and actuality continue to re-emerge in philosophical debates to the present day. Historians of philosophy analyze these universally significant metaphysical ideas to gain a better understanding of their meaning and practicing philosophers have rediscovered them and given them new life by using them in cutting-edge arguments.

The depth of its arguments and the complexity of its ideas suggest that Aristotle's *Metaphysics* has the potential to be found relevant to a wide range of philosophical debates that may emerge in the future.

---

1. Jonathan Barnes, *A Very Short Introduction to Aristotle* (Oxford: Oxford University Press, 2000), 136.
2. Edward Feser, "Introduction: An Aristotelian Revival?" in *Aristotle on Method and Metaphysics*, ed. Edward Feser (New York: Palgrave Macmillan, 2013), 2.
3. Jonathan Beere, *Doing and Being: An Interpretation of Aristotle's Metaphysics Theta* (Oxford: Oxford University Press, 2009).
4. Aristotle, *Metaphysics: Books Zeta and Eta*, trans. with commentary David Bostock (Oxford: Clarendon Press, 1994).
5. Joshua Hoffman and Gary S. Rosenkrantz, *Substance: Its Nature and Existence* (London and New York: Routledge, 1997).
6. Tuomas Tahko, "Metaphysics as the First Philosophy, " in *Aristotle on Method and Metaphysics*, ed. Edward Feser (New York: Palgrave Macmillan, 2013), 49–67.

GLOSSARY OF TERMS

1. **Academy:** philosophical school established by Aristotle's teacher Plato in the fourth century B.C.E.
2. **Accidental property:** a kind of property that is not essential to defining an object. For instance, a snub nose is an accidental property of a human being, because the shape of a nose varies from one person to another and thus it is not something that all humans fundamentally share.
3. **Actuality:** see Potentiality and actuality.
4. **Analytic philosophy:** branch of contemporary philosophy. Broadly speaking, the research methods of analytic philosophers differ from those of other philosophers with regard to their research methods—analytic philosophers base their research on logic and rigorous analysis.
5. **Antiquity:** the period before the Middle Ages, but within the span of Western human history.
6. **Apeiron:** a philosophical concept introduced by the pre-Socratic philosopher Anaximander. Literally meaning "limitless, " it denotes the idea that a fundamental creative principle exists that has peculiar generative properties not resembling the properties of any familiar elements.
7. **Athens:** the center of Greek philosophical learning at the time of Aristotle; Athens is one of the oldest cities in the world and has been inhabited for at least seven thousand years.
8. **Being qua being:** a phrase introduced by Aristotle, best understood as "being by virtue of being." Aristotle used it to describe his inquiry into being. It refers to investigating what we would today call ontology.
9. **Bundle theory:** a metaphysical theory that suggests that objects are best understood as collections—"bundles"—of all the properties they possess. This is alternative to the view that objects have special substantial properties that determine their identity.
10. **Christian:** a person who believes in the religion of Christianity, based on the teachings of Jesus Christ.
11. **Classical Greece:** a period in Greek culture lasting for around 200 years, from the fifth to the fourth century B.C.E.

| Glossary of Terms

12. **Cosmology:** study of the universe as a whole; in the context of ancient philosophy, it refers to the question of the origin of the world, the primary forces that are active in the world, and so on.
13. **Early modern period:** the period of history following the late Middle Ages, from around 1500 c.e. to around 1800 c.e.
14. **Empiricism:** the belief that knowledge is obtained on the basis of experience and observation.
15. **Enlightenment:** eighteenth-century intellectual movement marked by an emphasis on reason and a rejection of tradition.
16. **Essentialism:** the view that objects have certain core properties or characteristics that make up their identity.
17. **Exegesis:** the critical analysis and interpretation of a text.
18. **Hellenistic period:** the three centuries between the death of Alexander the Great and the rise of the ancient Roman Empire. This period is accepted as being between 323 b.c.e. and 31 b.c.e.
19. **Hylomorphism:** term that refers to the idea that substance is a form present in matter. Aristotle was the first to introduce this idea.
20. **Immanent form:** a form present in matter, as opposed to an independently existing form. Aristotle was the first to propose a theory involving this notion.
21. **Incorporeal:** an adjective that describes an object that has no physical body.
22. **Islam:** a religion whose followers worship Allah as the only God and believe in the prophet Muhammad.
23. **Logos:** a very popular—and notoriously hard to translate—concept among ancient philosophers. It typically refers to rationality of either a person or even the world itself. It plays a very important role in the thought of the pre-Socratic Greek philosopher Heraclitus, who argued that logos was the forming principle of the world.
24. **Lyceum:** philosophical school established by Aristotle in Athens in the fourth century b.c.e. Members of this school are known as Peripatetics.
25. **Macedonia:** a kingdom on the northern edge of Classical Greece. It was the

birthplace of Aristotle and Alexander the Great, who became its king.

26. **Medieval period:** also known as the Middle Ages, it is the period in European history that lasted from the fifth century C.E. to the fifteenth century C.E.

27. **Metaphysics:** subfield of philosophy that addresses the questions pertinent to existence, reality, or being itself.

28. **Metic:** term used to describe the social and political status of a person who resided in ancient Athens but was not a full citizen. Unlike citizens, metics could only partially participate in the political life, could not own land, and paid additional taxes.

29. **Middle Ages:** the period in European history that lasted from the fifth century C.E. to the fifteenth century C.E.

30. **Milesian school:** the earliest Greek school of thought, named after the town where it was founded (Miletus). The best-known members are Thales, Anaximander, and Anaximenes.

31. **Neoplatonists:** members of the Neoplatonic school of thought as established by Plotinus.

32. **Ontology:** subfield of metaphysics; it addresses questions relating to existence, such as "What exists in the world?, " "What types of existence are there?, " and "How can existences be grouped?"

33. **Partaking:** a standard philosophical term to describe how objects in the actual world interact with forms.

34. **Peripatetics:** the followers of Aristotle. It is said they were so named because the word derives from the Greek word for "walk" as Aristotle liked to walk around while he was delivering his lectures.

35. **Platonic:** relating to the work and thought of Plato.

36. **Platonism:** the philosophy of Plato.

37. **Potentiality and actuality:** Aristotelian concepts referring to modal states of objects. Potentiality refers to a possibility or capacity to change in a certain way, while actuality refers to the state when the capacity to change is fulfilled. An acorn,

for instance, is potentially an oak tree, but an oak tree exists as an actual substance.

38. **Pre-Socratics:** large group of Greek philosophers active before and during Socrates' lifetime (around 469 B.C.E. to 399 B.C.E.). These philosophers held very diverse views and are sometimes grouped into different schools, but they shared an interest in metaphysics and natural science.

39. **Renaissance:** meaning "rebirth," the period of history from the fourteenth to the seventeenth century C.E., marked by a revival of art and literature in Europe.

40. **Roman:** relating to the ancient Roman civilization that began on the Italian peninsula as early as the eighth century B.C.E. and lasted until the fifth century C.E. At the height of its power and influence in the first and second centuries C.E. it expanded to become an empire covering 6.5 million square kilometers (or 2.5 million square miles).

41. **Stoics:** an ancient philosophical school. The Stoics are especially famous for their radical ethical views, although they also presented a number of important metaphysical and epistemological arguments.

42. **Substance:** a philosophical concept denoting an object's essence, which differs from any accidental properties the object might have. The proponents of substance theory believe that the substance of a person is distinct, for instance, from that person being pale or having a snub nose. According to Aristotle, substance is an immanent form: that is, a form present in matter.

43. **Substantial property:** the kind of property that is essential to defining an object. A substantial property of a human being would be something that all human beings share and which is necessary for being human.

44. **Theory of Forms:** a theory that states that for every class of properties there is a universal form—an eternal, incorporeal entity that exists outside the actual world—which is both a perfect instance of that property and a cause of the existence of that property. For instance, human beings share the common property of being human in virtue of "partaking" in the Form of a Human Being.

45. **Third man argument:** an argument put forward by Aristotle that criticizes Plato's Theory of Forms. It shows that the forms cannot be the universals as their

own existence calls for a universal.

46. **Universal:** a philosophical concept denoting certain general common characteristics shared by all objects of the same kind. Its opposite is a particular, which refers to a specific individual of that kind. For instance, your pet dog is a particular instance of the universal "dog."

47. **Unmoved mover:** according to Aristotle this mover is the first cause of all change in the universe. It causes motion, but is not itself moved by any previous action. Aristotle considers whether there are many unmoved movers or just one, but his conclusion remains unclear.

PEOPLE MENTIONED IN THE TEXT

1. **John Ackrill (1921–2007)** was a British classicist and philosopher. He produced several important studies on Aristotle's philosophy.
2. **Alexander the Great (356–323 B.C.E.)** was a Macedonian king. He is best known for his vast military conquests. At its height, his empire stretched from the eastern part of the Mediterranean to the Himalayas.
3. **Alexander of Aphrodisias** was a Peripatetic commentator and philosopher who was active around the turn of the third century C.E. He is best known for writing commentaries on various works by Aristotle.
4. **Anaximander (c. 610–c. 546 B.C.E.)** was one of the Pre-Socratics in the Milesian school. He is best known for introducing the theory of apeiron ("limitless"), which suggests that the world is generated by an element-like entity not resembling any ordinary elements.
5. **Anaximenes (c. 585–c. 528 B.C.E.)** was one of the pre-Socratics in the Milesian school. He is best known for arguing that air was the foundational principle and material of the world.
6. **Andronicus of Rhodes** was a Peripatetic philosopher who is best known for editing and publishing Aristotle's works in the first century B.C.E. Very little is known about Andronicus himself and only fragments of his own works survive.
7. **Thomas Aquinas (1225–74 C.E.)** was one of the most important medieval philosopher-theologians. He wrote on most areas of philosophy, from metaphysics to ethics. His most famous works are *Summa Theologica* and *Summa contra Gentiles*.
8. **Averroes (Ibn Rushd) (1126–98 C.E.)** was an Islamic philosopher especially known for his commentaries on Aristotle.
9. **Avicenna (Ibn Sīnā) (980–1037 C.E.)** was a Persian philosopher and intellectual. He is especially well known for contributing to the development of medicine, but his philosophical work is also substantial. His ontological theories about being were strongly influenced by Aristotle.
10. **Jonathan Barnes (b. 1942)** is an emeritus professor of philosophy at the University of Oxford. He is one of the best-known contemporary experts of ancient

philosophy and has published numerous works on many ancient philosophers.

11. **Jonathan Beere** is a professor of ancient philosophy and history of science at the Humboldt-Universität zu Berlin. He specializes in ancient philosophy and has published a number of works on Aristotle's *Metaphysics*.

12. **David Bostock (b. 1936)** is an emeritus professor of philosophy at the University of Oxford. He has published many works on ancient philosophy, especially Plato and Aristotle.

13. **Baruch Brody (b. 1943)** is a professor of philosophy at Rice University in Texas. He is best known for his work in ethics, especially biomedical ethics.

14. **Thomas Case (1844–1925)** was a professor of moral and metaphysical philosophy at the University of Oxford. He is best known for his work in contemporary metaphysics, but he also produced several works on Aristotle.

15. **S. Marc Cohen** is an emeritus professor of philosophy at the University of Washington. He is an expert on ancient philosophy and has published many works on Aristotle.

16. **Demosthenes (384–322 B.C.E.)** was an orator and statesman in ancient Athens. He is especially well known for his political speeches.

17. **Empedocles (490–430 B.C.E.)** was a pre-Socratic philosopher and author of many notable doctrines. He is best known for being the first to advocate the four-element theory (fire, water, earth, air).

18. **Edward Feser (b. 1968)** is an associate professor of philosophy at Pasadena City College in Pasadena, California. He has published on a wide variety of topics in historical and contemporary philosophy.

19. **Lloyd Gerson** is a professor of philosophy at the University of Toronto. He is a noted expert who has published on many different topics in ancient philosophy.

20. **Ilsetraut Hadot** is an emerita professor at the French National Center for Scientific Research. She has published many works on ancient philosophy, especially Neoplatonism.

21. **Verity Harte** is a professor of philosophy and classics at Yale University. She is

a specialist in ancient philosophy, with particular interest in Plato and Aristotle.

22. **Heraclitus (535–475 B.C.E.)** was one of the best-known pre-Socratics. He argued that the world is governed by logos, a kind of rationality which he likened to fire.

23. **Joshua Hoffman** is a professor of philosophy at the University of North Carolina at Greensboro. He is known for his work on metaphysics and theology.

24. **David Hume (1711–76)** was an important Scottish philosopher, especially known for his philosophical empiricism, the main belief of which is that the principal source of knowledge is the senses.

25. **Terence Irwin (b. 1947)** is a professor of ancient philosophy at the University of Oxford. He is an expert on ancient philosophy and the history of ethics.

26. **Anthony Kenny (b. 1931)** is an emeritus professor of philosophy at the University of Oxford. He is a noted expert on ancient philosophy and Aristotle.

27. **Claude Panaccio (b. 1946)** is a professor of philosophy at the University of Quebec. He is an expert in medieval philosophy.

28. **Parmenides (late sixth or early fifth century B.C.E.)** was a pre-Socratic philosopher, the founder of the Eleatic school of philosophy. He is known for the controversial theory of reality found in his fragmentary poem "On Nature."

29. **Plato (429–347 B.C.E.)** was a Greek philosopher who is one of the most important figures in the history of philosophy. His best-known works are the dialogues *Republic*, *Timaeus*, and *Apology*.

30. **Plotinus (204–70 C.E.)** was the founder of the Neoplatonic philosophical school. He is known for creating a complex but well-rounded philosophical system preserved in a work called *Enneads*.

31. **Gary Rosenkrantz** is a professor of philosophy at the University of North Carolina at Greensboro. He is known for his work on metaphysics and theological issues.

32. **Theodore Scaltsas (b. 1949)** is a professor of philosophy at the University of Edinburgh. He works on ancient philosophy and contemporary metaphysics.

33. **David Sedley (b. 1947)** is a professor of ancient philosophy at the University of Cambridge. He is a very well-known scholar who has worked on many areas of ancient philosophy.

34. **Robert Sharples (1949–2010)** was a professor in the Greek and Latin department at University College London during an extensive career and was well-respected for his work on Ancient Greek philosophy.

35. **Christopher Shields** is a professor of philosophy at the University of Notre Dame. He is an expert on ancient philosophy and has written extensively on Aristotle.

36. **Socrates (470/469–399 B.C.E.)** was a Greek philosopher, and one of the most important figures in the Western philosophical tradition. He is known for his rigorous philosophical questioning methods and interest in ethical questions. Socrates left no written works, so all we know of him comes from the writing of his pupils, most notably Plato.

37. **Tuomas Tahko** is an associate professor of philosophy at the University of Helsinki. He specializes in contemporary metaphysics.

38. **Thales (c. 624–c. 546 B.C.E.)** was one of the pre-Socratics in the Milesian school, typically referred to as the first philosopher in the Greek tradition. He is best known for arguing that water was the founding principle and material of the world.

WORKS CITED

1. Ackrill, J. L. *Aristotle the Philosopher*. Oxford: Oxford University Press, 1981.
2. Annas, Julia. *Ancient Philosophy: A Very Short Introduction*. Oxford: Oxford University Press, 2000.
3. Aristotle. *Categories*. Translated by John L. Ackrill. In vol. 1 of *The Complete Works of Aristotle: The Revised Oxford Translation*, edited by Jonathan Barnes, 3–24. Princeton, NJ: Princeton University Press, 1984.
4. *Metaphysics*. Translated by William David Ross. In vol. 2 of *The Complete Works of Aristotle: The Revised Oxford Translation*, edited by Jonathan Barnes, 1552–728. Princeton, NJ: Princeton University Press, 1984.
5. *Metaphysics: Books Gamma, Delta, and Epsilon*. Translated with notes by Christopher Kirwan. Oxford: Clarendon Press, 1993.
6. *Metaphysics: Books Zeta and Eta*. Translated with a commentary by David Bostock. Oxford: Clarendon Press, 1994.
7. Barnes, Jonathan. *A Very Short Introduction to Aristotle*. Oxford: Oxford University Press, 2000.
8. "Life and work." In *The Cambridge Companion to Aristotle*, edited by Jonathan Barnes, 1–26. Cambridge: Cambridge University Press, 1995.
9. "Metaphysics." In *The Cambridge Companion to Aristotle*, edited by Jonathan Barnes, 66–108. Cambridge: Cambridge University Press, 1995.
10. "Roman Aristotle." In *Philosophia Togata* II, *Plato and Aristotle at Rome*, edited by Jonathan Barnes and Miriam Griffin. Oxford: Clarendon Press, 1997.
11. Beere, Jonathan. *Doing and Being: An Interpretation of Aristotle's Metaphysics Theta*. Oxford: Oxford University Press, 2009.
12. Bradley, F. H. *Appearance and Reality: A Metaphysical Essay*. London: S. Sonnenschein; New York: Macmillan, 1893.
13. Case, Thomas. "Aristotle." In *Aristotle's Philosophical Development: Problems and Prospects*, edited by William Wians, 1–40. Lanham, MD: Rowman & Littlefield, 1996.
14. Code, Alan. "Aristotle's Logic and Metaphysics." In *Routledge History of Philosophy, Volume II: From Aristotle to Augustine*, edited by David Furley,

40–75. London: Routledge, 1999.

15. Cohen, S. Marc. "Substances." In *A Companion to Aristotle*, edited by Georgios Anagnostopoulos, 197–213. Malden, MA: Wiley-Blackwell, 2009.

16. Feser, Edward. "Introduction: An Aristotelian Revival?" *In Aristotle on Method and Metaphysics*, edited by Edward Feser, 1–6. New York: Palgrave Macmillan, 2013.

17. Furley, David. Introduction to *Routledge History of Philosophy, Volume II: From Aristotle to Augustine*, edited by David Furley, 1–8. London: Routledge, 1999.

18. Gerson, Lloyd. *Plotinus*. London and New York: Routledge, 1994.

19. Guthrie, W. K. C. *The Greek Philosophers: From Thales to Aristotle*. London: Routledge, 2013.

20. Hadot, Ilsetraut. "The Role of the Commentaries on Aristotle in the Teaching of Philosophy According to the Prefaces of the Neoplatonic Commentaries on the *Categories*." *Oxford Studies of Ancient Philosophy* supplementary volume (1991): 175–89.

21. Harte, Verity. "Plato's Metaphysics." In *The Oxford Handbook of Plato*, edited by Gail Fine, 191–216.Oxford: Oxford University Press, 2008.

22. Hoffman, Joshua, and Gary S. Rosenkrantz. *Substance: Its Nature and Existence*. London and New York: Routledge, 1997.

23. Huggett, Nick. "Zeno's Paradoxes." *Stanford Encyclopedia of Philosophy*. Accessed February 11, 2015. http: //plato.stanford.edu/entries/paradox-zeno/.

24. Irwin, Terence. "Aristotle." In *The Shorter Routledge Encyclopedia of Philosophy*, edited by Edward Craig, 50–67. London: Routledge, 2005.

25. Irwin, Terence, and Gail Fine. *Aristotle: Introductory Readings*. Indianapolis, IN: Hackett Publishing Company, 1996.

26. Kenny, Anthony. *Ancient Philosophy: A New History of Western Philosophy*. Oxford: Oxford University Press, 2006.

27. Kretzmann, Norman, and Eleonore Stump. "Thomas Aquinas." In *The Shorter Routledge Encyclopedia of Philosophy*, edited by Edward Craig, 30–48. London: Routledge, 2005.

28. Lear, Jonathan. *Aristotle: The Desire to Understand*. Cambridge: Cambridge University Press, 1988.

29. Loux, Michael. *Primary "Ousia": An Essay on Aristotle's Metaphysics Z and H.*

Ithaca, NY: Cornell University Press, 1991.

30. Panaccio, Claude. "Medieval Metaphysics 1: The Problem of Universals." In *The Routledge Companion to Metaphysics*, edited by Robin Le Poidevin, Peter Simons, Andrew McGonigal, and Ross P. Cameron, 48–57. London and New York: Routledge, 2009.

31. Plato. *Phaedo*. Translated by G. M. A. Grube. In *Plato: Complete Works*, edited by John M. Cooper, 49–100. Indianapolis, IN; Cambridge: Hackett Publishing Company, 1997.

32. *Sophist*. Translated by Nicholas P. White. In *Plato: Complete Works*, edited by John M. Cooper, 235–293. Indianapolis, IN; Cambridge: Hackett Publishing Company, 1997.

33. Rizvi, Sajjad H. "Avicenna (Ibn Sīnā)." Internet Encyclopedia of Philosophy. Accessed February 11, 2015. http://www.iep.utm.edu/avicenna/.

34. Robinson, Howard. "Substance." *Stanford Encyclopedia of Philosophy*. Accessed February 10, 2015. http://plato.stanford.edu/entries/substance/.

35. Sachs, Joe. "Aristotle: Metaphysics." Internet Encyclopedia of Philosophy. Accessed February 10, 2015. http://www.iep.utm.edu/aris-met/.

36. Scaltsas, Theodore. *Substances and Universals in Aristotle's Metaphysics*. New York: Cornell University Press, 1994.

37. Sharples, Robert. "The Peripatetic School." In *Routledge History of Philosophy, Volume II: From Aristotle to Augustine*, edited by David Furley, 147–87. London and New York: Routledge, 1999.

38. Shields, Christopher. *Aristotle*. London: Routledge, 2007.

39. "Aristotle." *Stanford Encyclopedia of Philosophy*. Accessed February 10, 2015. http://plato.stanford.edu/entries/aristotle/.

40. "Aristotle's Philosophical Life and Writing." In *The Oxford Handbook of Aristotle*, edited by Christopher Shields, 3–16. Oxford: Oxford University Press, 2012.

41. Tahko, Tuomas. "Metaphysics as the First Philosophy." In *Aristotle on Method and Metaphysics*, edited by Edward Feser, 49–67. New York: Palgrave Macmillan, 2013.

42. Thom, Paul. "Logical Form." In *The Oxford Handbook of Medieval Philosophy*, edited by John Marenbon, 271–88. Oxford: Oxford University Press, 2012.

原书作者简介

亚里士多德于公元前 384 年出生于今天的马其顿。17 岁时，他搬到希腊雅典，跟随柏拉图在其著名的阿加德米学园学习哲学，后者是欧洲哲学的创始人之一。公元前 347 年柏拉图去世后，亚里士多德返回马其顿，为年轻的亚历山大大帝授课。公元前 335 年，他再次来到雅典，并建立了自己的学校吕克昂学园。政治骚乱迫使亚里士多德在公元前 322 年再次离开雅典，此后不久他在埃维亚岛去世。

本书作者简介

艾斯泰·塞尔凯特博士，专事古典哲学的研究者。现为韩国延世大学博士后研究员。

世界名著中的批判性思维

《世界思想宝库钥匙丛书》致力于深入浅出地阐释全世界著名思想家的观点，不论是谁、在何处都能了解到，从而推进批判性思维发展。

《世界思想宝库钥匙丛书》与世界顶尖大学的一流学者合作，为一系列学科中最有影响的著作推出新的分析文本，介绍其观点和影响。在这一不断扩展的系列中，每种选入的著作都代表了历经时间考验的思想典范。通过为这些著作提供必要背景、揭示原作者的学术渊源以及说明这些著作所产生的影响，本系列图书希望让读者以新视角看待这些划时代的经典之作。读者应学会思考、运用并挑战这些著作中的观点，而不是简单接受它们。

ABOUT THE AUTHOR OF THE ORIGINAL WORK

Aristotle was born in 384 BCE in what is present-day Macedonia. At the age of 17, he moved to Athens in Greece to begin an education in philosophy under Plato, one of the founders of European philosophy, at his renowned Academy. On Plato's death in 347 BCE, Aristotle moved back to Macedonia to tutor the young Alexander the Great. But in 335 BCE he returned to Athens and established his own school, the Lyceum. Political unrest forced Aristotle to leave Athens again in 322 BCE, and he died shortly afterwards on the island of Euboea.

ABOUT THE AUTHOR OF THE ANALYSIS

Dr Aiste Celkyte is a researcher specialising in ancient philosophy. She is currently a postdoctoral researcher at Yonsei University in South Korea.

ABOUT MACAT
GREAT WORKS FOR CRITICAL THINKING

Macat is focused on making the ideas of the world's great thinkers accessible and comprehensible to everybody, everywhere, in ways that promote the development of enhanced critical thinking skills.

It works with leading academics from the world's top universities to produce new analyses that focus on the ideas and the impact of the most influential works ever written across a wide variety of academic disciplines. Each of the works that sit at the heart of its growing library is an enduring example of great thinking. But by setting them in context — and looking at the influences that shaped their authors, as well as the responses they provoked — Macat encourages readers to look at these classics and game-changers with fresh eyes. Readers learn to think, engage and challenge their ideas, rather than simply accepting them.

批判性思维与《形而上学》

首要批判性思维技巧：理性化思维

次要批判性思维技巧：分析、阐释、评估

　　亚里士多德的《形而上学》是涉及广泛主题的文集，几乎可以肯定该书并非由亚氏自己结集成册，这也解释了为什么该书能涉及如此广泛的材料，从意义到数学，从逻辑序列到宗教。它包括极其有用的对公理（或首要真理）的解析，如矛盾律和逻辑定律。

　　在审视这些内容时，亚里士多德为清晰的思维提供了持续指导，这将在对论点的分析和评估以及良好推理的产生中得到证明。为对阐释提供有价值的讨论，他还观察同音异义词（如"这把刀很锋利（sharp）"和"这个注释很尖刻（sharp）"），以及介于同音异义词和同义词之间的他所谓的"同源词"（如"健康的"一词）。《形而上学》对研究有益，其中常有假设推理的例子，如在数学（"如果 x，则 y……"）和科学（"如果 a 移动 b，b 移动 c……则什么移动 a？"）中的使用。此外，亚里士多德分析了柏拉图的论点，对它们进行持续的（批判性）评估。《形而上学》表明亚里士多德构建了许多发展良好的批判性思维模式，它首先是一部关于精妙推理的著作，其中所创造的强有力的论点，在成书后2 500年的今天，仍不断被辩论和运用。

CRITICAL THINKING AND *METAPHYSICS*

- Primary critical thinking skill: REASONING
- Secondary critical thinking skill: ANALYSIS, INTERPRETATION, EVALUATION

Aristotle's *Metaphysics* is a collection of essays on a wide range of topics, almost certainly never put together by Aristotle himself. This helps to explain why the material covers such a very wide range of material, from meaning to mathematics, from logical sequences to religion. It includes very useful treatments of the nature of axioms (or primary truths) such as the law of non-contradiction and the laws of logic.

In looking at these, Aristotle provides sustained guides to clear thinking as would be evidenced in analysis and evaluation of arguments and the production of good reasoning. He also provides some valuable discussion of interpretation by looking at homonyms (as in 'this knife is sharp' and 'this note is sharp') and what he calls 'paronyms,' which lie between homonyms and synonyms: an example is the word 'healthy'. *Metaphysics* is also useful to study for its frequent examples of hypothetical reasoning, including their use in mathematics ('if x, then y...') and science ('if a moves b, then b moves c...', so what moves a?). In addition, we find Aristotle analysing Plato's arguments and subjecting them to sustained (critical) evaluation. While *Metaphysics* shows Aristotle in many well-developed critical thinking modes, it is first and foremost a work of exquisite reasoning, creating strong arguments that continue to be debated and deployed today, nearly 2500 years after they were written.

《世界思想宝库钥匙丛书》简介

《世界思想宝库钥匙丛书》致力于为一系列在各领域产生重大影响的人文社科类经典著作提供独特的学术探讨。每一本读物都不仅仅是原经典著作的内容摘要,而是介绍并深入研究原经典著作的学术渊源、主要观点和历史影响。这一丛书的目的是提供一套学习资料,以促进读者掌握批判性思维,从而更全面、深刻地去理解重要思想。

每一本读物分为3个部分:学术渊源、学术思想和学术影响,每个部分下有4个小节。这些章节旨在从各个方面研究原经典著作及其反响。

由于独特的体例,每一本读物不但易于阅读,而且另有一项优点:所有读物的编排体例相同,读者在进行某个知识层面的调查或研究时可交叉参阅多本该丛书中的相关读物,从而开启跨领域研究的路径。

为了方便阅读,每本读物最后还列出了术语表和人名表(在书中则以星号 * 标记),此外还有参考文献。

《世界思想宝库钥匙丛书》与剑桥大学合作,理清了批判性思维的要点,即如何通过6种技能来进行有效思考。其中3种技能让我们能够理解问题,另3种技能让我们有能力解决问题。这6种技能合称为"批判性思维 PACIER 模式",它们是:

分析:了解如何建立一个观点;
评估:研究一个观点的优点和缺点;
阐释:对意义所产生的问题加以理解;
创造性思维:提出新的见解,发现新的联系;
解决问题:提出切实有效的解决办法;
理性化思维:创建有说服力的观点。

THE MACAT LIBRARY

The Macat Library is a series of unique academic explorations of seminal works in the humanities and social sciences — books and papers that have had a significant and widely recognised impact on their disciplines. It has been created to serve as much more than just a summary of what lies between the covers of a great book. It illuminates and explores the influences on, ideas of, and impact of that book. Our goal is to offer a learning resource that encourages critical thinking and fosters a better, deeper understanding of important ideas.

Each publication is divided into three Sections: Influences, Ideas, and Impact. Each Section has four Modules. These explore every important facet of the work, and the responses to it.

This Section-Module structure makes a Macat Library book easy to use, but it has another important feature. Because each Macat book is written to the same format, it is possible (and encouraged!) to cross-reference multiple Macat books along the same lines of inquiry or research. This allows the reader to open up interesting interdisciplinary pathways.

To further aid your reading, lists of glossary terms and people mentioned are included at the end of this book (these are indicated by an asterisk [*] throughout) — as well as a list of works cited.

Macat has worked with the University of Cambridge to identify the elements of critical thinking and understand the ways in which six different skills combine to enable effective thinking.

Three allow us to fully understand a problem; three more give us the tools to solve it. Together, these six skills make up the PACIER model of critical thinking. They are:

ANALYSIS — understanding how an argument is built
EVALUATION — exploring the strengths and weaknesses of an argument
INTERPRETATION — understanding issues of meaning
CREATIVE THINKING — coming up with new ideas and fresh connections
PROBLEM-SOLVING — producing strong solutions
REASONING — creating strong arguments

"《世界思想宝库钥匙丛书》提供了独一无二的跨学科学习和研究工具。它介绍那些革新了各自学科研究的经典著作,还邀请全世界一流专家和教育机构进行严谨的分析,为每位读者打开世界顶级教育的大门。"

—— 安德烈亚斯·施莱歇尔,
经济合作与发展组织教育与技能司司长

"《世界思想宝库钥匙丛书》直面大学教育的巨大挑战……他们组建了一支精干而活跃的学者队伍,来推出在研究广度上颇具新意的教学材料。"

—— 布罗尔斯教授、勋爵,剑桥大学前校长

"《世界思想宝库钥匙丛书》的愿景令人赞叹。它通过分析和阐释那些曾深刻影响人类思想以及社会、经济发展的经典文本,提供了新的学习方法。它推动批判性思维,这对于任何社会和经济体来说都是至关重要的。这就是未来的学习方法。"

—— 查尔斯·克拉克阁下,英国前教育大臣

"对于那些影响了各自领域的著作,《世界思想宝库钥匙丛书》能让人们立即了解到围绕那些著作展开的评论性言论,这让该系列图书成为在这些领域从事研究的师生们不可或缺的资源。"

—— 威廉·特朗佐教授,加利福尼亚大学圣地亚哥分校

"Macat offers an amazing first-of-its-kind tool for interdisciplinary learning and research. Its focus on works that transformed their disciplines and its rigorous approach, drawing on the world's leading experts and educational institutions, opens up a world-class education to anyone."

—— Andreas Schleicher, Director for Education and Skills, Organisation for Economic Co-operation and Development

"Macat is taking on some of the major challenges in university education... They have drawn together a strong team of active academics who are producing teaching materials that are novel in the breadth of their approach."

—— Prof Lord Broers, former Vice-Chancellor of the University of Cambridge

"The Macat vision is exceptionally exciting. It focuses upon new modes of learning which analyse and explain seminal texts which have profoundly influenced world thinking and so social and economic development. It promotes the kind of critical thinking which is essential for any society and economy. This is the learning of the future."

—— Rt Hon Charles Clarke, former UK Secretary of State for Education

"The Macat analyses provide immediate access to the critical conversation surrounding the books that have shaped their respective discipline, which will make them an invaluable resource to all of those, students and teachers, working in the field."

—— Prof William Tronzo, University of California at San Diego

The Macat Library
世界思想宝库钥匙丛书

TITLE	中文书名	类别
An Analysis of Arjun Appadurai's *Modernity at Large: Cultural Dimensions of Globalization*	解析阿尔君·阿帕杜莱《消失的现代性：全球化的文化维度》	人类学
An Analysis of Claude Lévi-Strauss's *Structural Anthropology*	解析克劳德·列维-斯特劳斯《结构人类学》	人类学
An Analysis of Marcel Mauss's *The Gift*	解析马塞尔·莫斯《礼物》	人类学
An Analysis of Jared M. Diamond's *Guns, Germs, and Steel: The Fate of Human Societies*	解析贾雷德·M.戴蒙德《枪炮、病菌与钢铁：人类社会的命运》	人类学
An Analysis of Clifford Geertz's *The Interpretation of Cultures*	解析克利福德·格尔茨《文化的解释》	人类学
An Analysis of Philippe Ariès's *Centuries of Childhood: A Social History of Family Life*	解析菲力浦·阿利埃斯《儿童的世纪：旧制度下的儿童和家庭生活》	人类学
An Analysis of W. Chan Kim & Renée Mauborgne's *Blue Ocean Strategy*	解析金伟灿/勒妮·莫博涅《蓝海战略》	商业
An Analysis of John P. Kotter's *Leading Change*	解析约翰·P.科特《领导变革》	商业
An Analysis of Michael E. Porter's *Competitive Strategy: Techniques for Analyzing Industries and Competitors*	解析迈克尔·E.波特《竞争战略：分析产业和竞争对手的技术》	商业
An Analysis of Jean Lave & Etienne Wenger's *Situated Learning: Legitimate Peripheral Participation*	解析琼·莱夫/艾蒂纳·温格《情境学习：合法的边缘性参与》	商业
An Analysis of Douglas McGregor's *The Human Side of Enterprise*	解析道格拉斯·麦格雷戈《企业的人性面》	商业
An Analysis of Milton Friedman's *Capitalism and Freedom*	解析米尔顿·弗里德曼《资本主义与自由》	商业
An Analysis of Ludwig von Mises's *The Theory of Money and Credit*	解析路德维希·冯·米塞斯《货币和信用理论》	经济学
An Analysis of Adam Smith's *The Wealth of Nations*	解析亚当·斯密《国富论》	经济学
An Analysis of Thomas Piketty's *Capital in the Twenty-First Century*	解析托马斯·皮凯蒂《21世纪资本论》	经济学
An Analysis of Nassim Nicholas Taleb's *The Black Swan: The Impact of the Highly Improbable*	解析纳西姆·尼古拉斯·塔勒布《黑天鹅：如何应对不可预知的未来》	经济学
An Analysis of Ha-Joon Chang's *Kicking Away the Ladder*	解析张夏准《富国陷阱：发达国家为何踢开梯子》	经济学
An Analysis of Thomas Robert Malthus's *An Essay on the Principle of Population*	解析托马斯·罗伯特·马尔萨斯《人口论》	经济学

An Analysis of John Maynard Keynes's *The General Theory of Employment, Interest and Money*	解析约翰·梅纳德·凯恩斯《就业、利息和货币通论》	经济学
An Analysis of Milton Friedman's *The Role of Monetary Policy*	解析米尔顿·弗里德曼《货币政策的作用》	经济学
An Analysis of Burton G. Malkiel's *A Random Walk Down Wall Street*	解析伯顿·G.马尔基尔《漫步华尔街》	经济学
An Analysis of Friedrich A. Hayek's *The Road to Serfdom*	解析弗里德里希·A.哈耶克《通往奴役之路》	经济学
An Analysis of Charles P. Kindleberger's *Manias, Panics, and Crashes: A History of Financial Crises*	解析查尔斯·P.金德尔伯格《疯狂、惊恐和崩溃:金融危机史》	经济学
An Analysis of Amartya Sen's *Development as Freedom*	解析阿马蒂亚·森《以自由看待发展》	经济学
An Analysis of Rachel Carson's *Silent Spring*	解析蕾切尔·卡森《寂静的春天》	地理学
An Analysis of Charles Darwin's *On the Origin of Species: by Means of Natural Selection, or The Preservation of Favoured Races in the Struggle for Life*	解析查尔斯·达尔文《物种起源》	地理学
An Analysis of World Commission on Environment and Development's *The Brundtland Report: Our Common Future*	解析世界环境与发展委员会《布伦特兰报告:我们共同的未来》	地理学
An Analysis of James E. Lovelock's *Gaia: A New Look at Life on Earth*	解析詹姆斯·E.拉伍洛克《盖娅:地球生命的新视野》	地理学
An Analysis of Paul Kennedy's *The Rise and Fall of the Great Powers: Economic Change and Military Conflict from 1500–2000*	解析保罗·肯尼迪《大国的兴衰:1500—2000年的经济变革与军事冲突》	历史
An Analysis of Janet L. Abu-Lughod's *Before European Hegemony: The World System A. D. 1250–1350*	解析珍妮特·L.阿布-卢格霍德《欧洲霸权之前:1250—1350年的世界体系》	历史
An Analysis of Alfred W. Crosby's *The Columbian Exchange: Biological and Cultural Consequences of 1492*	解析艾尔弗雷德·W.克罗斯比《哥伦布大交换:1492年以后的生物影响和文化冲击》	历史
An Analysis of Tony Judt's *Postwar: A History of Europe since 1945*	解析托尼·朱特《战后欧洲史》	历史
An Analysis of Richard J. Evans's *In Defence of History*	解析理查德·J.艾文斯《捍卫历史》	历史
An Analysis of Eric Hobsbawm's *The Age of Revolution: Europe 1789–1848*	解析艾瑞克·霍布斯鲍姆《革命的年代:欧洲1789—1848年》	历史

An Analysis of Roland Barthes's *Mythologies*	解析罗兰·巴特《神话学》	文学与批判理论
An Analysis of Simone de Beauvoir's *The Second Sex*	解析西蒙娜·德·波伏娃《第二性》	文学与批判理论
An Analysis of Edward W. Said's *Orientalism*	解析爱德华·W. 萨义德《东方主义》	文学与批判理论
An Analysis of Virginia Woolf's *A Room of One's Own*	解析弗吉尼亚·伍尔芙《一间自己的房间》	文学与批判理论
An Analysis of Judith Butler's *Gender Trouble*	解析朱迪斯·巴特勒《性别麻烦》	文学与批判理论
An Analysis of Ferdinand de Saussure's *Course in General Linguistics*	解析费尔迪南·德·索绪尔《普通语言学教程》	文学与批判理论
An Analysis of Susan Sontag's *On Photography*	解析苏珊·桑塔格《论摄影》	文学与批判理论
An Analysis of Walter Benjamin's *The Work of Art in the Age of Mechanical Reproduction*	解析瓦尔特·本雅明《机械复制时代的艺术作品》	文学与批判理论
An Analysis of W. E. B. Du Bois's *The Souls of Black Folk*	解析W.E.B. 杜波依斯《黑人的灵魂》	文学与批判理论
An Analysis of Plato's *The Republic*	解析柏拉图《理想国》	哲学
An Analysis of Plato's *Symposium*	解析柏拉图《会饮篇》	哲学
An Analysis of Aristotle's *Metaphysics*	解析亚里士多德《形而上学》	哲学
An Analysis of Aristotle's *Nicomachean Ethics*	解析亚里士多德《尼各马可伦理学》	哲学
An Analysis of Immanuel Kant's *Critique of Pure Reason*	解析伊曼努尔·康德《纯粹理性批判》	哲学
An Analysis of Ludwig Wittgenstein's *Philosophical Investigations*	解析路德维希·维特根斯坦《哲学研究》	哲学
An Analysis of G. W. F. Hegel's *Phenomenology of Spirit*	解析G.W.F. 黑格尔《精神现象学》	哲学
An Analysis of Baruch Spinoza's *Ethics*	解析巴鲁赫·斯宾诺莎《伦理学》	哲学
An Analysis of Hannah Arendt's *The Human Condition*	解析汉娜·阿伦特《人的境况》	哲学
An Analysis of G. E. M. Anscombe's *Modern Moral Philosophy*	解析G.E.M. 安斯康姆《现代道德哲学》	哲学
An Analysis of David Hume's *An Enquiry Concerning Human Understanding*	解析大卫·休谟《人类理解研究》	哲学

An Analysis of Søren Kierkegaard's *Fear and Trembling*	解析索伦·克尔凯郭尔《恐惧与战栗》	哲学
An Analysis of René Descartes's *Meditations on First Philosophy*	解析勒内·笛卡尔《第一哲学沉思录》	哲学
An Analysis of Friedrich Nietzsche's *On the Genealogy of Morality*	解析弗里德里希·尼采《论道德的谱系》	哲学
An Analysis of Gilbert Ryle's *The Concept of Mind*	解析吉尔伯特·赖尔《心的概念》	哲学
An Analysis of Thomas Kuhn's *The Structure of Scientific Revolutions*	解析托马斯·库恩《科学革命的结构》	哲学
An Analysis of John Stuart Mill's *Utilitarianism*	解析约翰·斯图亚特·穆勒《功利主义》	哲学
An Analysis of Aristotle's *Politics*	解析亚里士多德《政治学》	政治学
An Analysis of Niccolò Machiavelli's *The Prince*	解析尼科洛·马基雅维利《君主论》	政治学
An Analysis of Karl Marx's *Capital*	解析卡尔·马克思《资本论》	政治学
An Analysis of Benedict Anderson's *Imagined Communities*	解析本尼迪克特·安德森《想象的共同体》	政治学
An Analysis of Samuel P. Huntington's *The Clash of Civilizations and the Remaking of World Order*	解析塞缪尔·P.亨廷顿《文明的冲突与世界秩序的重建》	政治学
An Analysis of Alexis de Tocqueville's *Democracy in America*	解析阿列克西·德·托克维尔《论美国的民主》	政治学
An Analysis of John A. Hobson's *Imperialism: A Study*	解析约翰·A.霍布森《帝国主义》	政治学
An Analysis of Thomas Paine's *Common Sense*	解析托马斯·潘恩《常识》	政治学
An Analysis of John Rawls's *A Theory of Justice*	解析约翰·罗尔斯《正义论》	政治学
An Analysis of Francis Fukuyama's *The End of History and the Last Man*	解析弗朗西斯·福山《历史的终结与最后的人》	政治学
An Analysis of John Locke's *Two Treatises of Government*	解析约翰·洛克《政府论》	政治学
An Analysis of Sun Tzu's *The Art of War*	解析孙武《孙子兵法》	政治学
An Analysis of Henry Kissinger's *World Order: Reflections on the Character of Nations and the Course of History*	解析亨利·基辛格《世界秩序》	政治学
An Analysis of Jean-Jacques Rousseau's *The Social Contract*	解析让-雅克·卢梭《社会契约论》	政治学

English Title	Chinese Title	学科
An Analysis of Odd Arne Westad's *The Global Cold War: Third World Interventions and the Making of Our Times*	解析文安立《全球冷战：美苏对第三世界的干涉与当代世界的形成》	政治学
An Analysis of Sigmund Freud's *The Interpretation of Dreams*	解析西格蒙德·弗洛伊德《梦的解析》	心理学
An Analysis of William James' *The Principles of Psychology*	解析威廉·詹姆斯《心理学原理》	心理学
An Analysis of Philip Zimbardo's *The Lucifer Effect*	解析菲利普·津巴多《路西法效应》	心理学
An Analysis of Leon Festinger's *A Theory of Cognitive Dissonance*	解析利昂·费斯汀格《认知失调论》	心理学
An Analysis of Richard H. Thaler & Cass R. Sunstein's *Nudge: Improving Decisions about Health, Wealth, and Happiness*	解析理查德·H. 泰勒/卡斯·R. 桑斯坦《助推：如何做出有关健康、财富和幸福的更优决策》	心理学
An Analysis of Gordon Allport's *The Nature of Prejudice*	解析高尔登·奥尔波特《偏见的本质》	心理学
An Analysis of Steven Pinker's *The Better Angels of Our Nature: Why Violence Has Declined*	解析斯蒂芬·平克《人性中的善良天使：暴力为什么会减少》	心理学
An Analysis of Stanley Milgram's *Obedience to Authority*	解析斯坦利·米尔格拉姆《对权威的服从》	心理学
An Analysis of Betty Friedan's *The Feminine Mystique*	解析贝蒂·弗里丹《女性的奥秘》	心理学
An Analysis of David Riesman's *The Lonely Crowd: A Study of the Changing American Character*	解析大卫·理斯曼《孤独的人群：美国人社会性格演变之研究》	社会学
An Analysis of Franz Boas's *Race, Language and Culture*	解析弗朗兹·博厄斯《种族、语言与文化》	社会学
An Analysis of Pierre Bourdieu's *Outline of a Theory of Practice*	解析皮埃尔·布尔迪厄《实践理论大纲》	社会学
An Analysis of Max Weber's *The Protestant Ethic and the Spirit of Capitalism*	解析马克斯·韦伯《新教伦理与资本主义精神》	社会学
An Analysis of Jane Jacobs' *The Death and Life of Great American Cities*	解析简·雅各布斯《美国大城市的死与生》	社会学
An Analysis of C. Wright Mills's *The Sociological Imagination*	解析C. 赖特·米尔斯《社会学的想象力》	社会学
An Analysis of Robert E. Lucas Jr.'s *Why Doesn't Capital Flow from Rich to Poor Countries?*	解析小罗伯特·E. 卢卡斯《为何资本不从富国流向穷国？》	社会学

An Analysis of Émile Durkheim's *On Suicide*	解析埃米尔·迪尔凯姆《自杀论》	社会学
An Analysis of Eric Hoffer's *The True Believer: Thoughts on the Nature of Mass Movements*	解析埃里克·霍弗《狂热分子：群众运动圣经》	社会学
An Analysis of Jared M. Diamond's *Collapse: How Societies Choose to Fail or Survive*	解析贾雷德·M.戴蒙德《大崩溃：社会如何选择兴亡》	社会学
An Analysis of Michel Foucault's *The History of Sexuality Vol. 1: The Will to Knowledge*	解析米歇尔·福柯《性史（第一卷）：求知意志》	社会学
An Analysis of Michel Foucault's *Discipline and Punish*	解析米歇尔·福柯《规训与惩罚》	社会学
An Analysis of Richard Dawkins's *The Selfish Gene*	解析理查德·道金斯《自私的基因》	社会学
An Analysis of Antonio Gramsci's *Prison Notebooks*	解析安东尼奥·葛兰西《狱中札记》	社会学
An Analysis of Augustine's *Confessions*	解析奥古斯丁《忏悔录》	神学
An Analysis of C. S. Lewis's *The Abolition of Man*	解析 C. S. 路易斯《人之废》	神学

图书在版编目（CIP）数据

解析亚里士多德《形而上学》：汉、英 / 艾斯泰·塞尔凯特（Aiste Celkyte）著；宫昀译. —上海：上海外语教育出版社，2021
（世界思想宝库钥匙丛书）
ISBN 978-7-5446-6671-8

Ⅰ.①解… Ⅱ.①艾… ②宫… Ⅲ.①亚里士多德（Aristotle 前384-前322）－形而上学－研究－汉、英 Ⅳ.①B081.1 ②B502.233

中国版本图书馆CIP数据核字（2021）第028849号

This Chinese-English bilingual edition of *An Analysis of Aristotle's* Metaphysics is published by arrangement with Macat International Limited.
Licensed for sale throughout the world.

本书汉英双语版由Macat国际有限公司授权上海外语教育出版社有限公司出版。供在全世界范围内发行、销售。

图字：09 – 2018 – 549

出版发行：上海外语教育出版社
（上海外国语大学内） 邮编：200083
电　　话： 021-65425300（总机）
电子邮箱： bookinfo@sflep.com.cn
网　　址： http://www.sflep.com
责任编辑： 李振荣

印　　刷： 上海宝山译文印刷厂有限公司
开　　本： 890×1240 1/32 印张 5.625 字数 115千字
版　　次： 2021年7月第1版 2021年7月第1次印刷
书　　号： ISBN 978-7-5446-6671-8
定　　价： 30.00 元

本版图书如有印装质量问题，可向本社调换
质量服务热线: 4008-213-263 电子邮箱: editorial@sflep.com